RETIRE
EARLY AND
WEALTHY

RETIRE EARLY AND WEALTHY

7 STEPS TO WISDOM AND FINANCIAL FREEDOM

DAVID SINGH

ECW PRESS

Published by ECW PRESS
2120 Queen Street East, Suite 200, Toronto, Ontario, Canada M4E 1E2

LIBRARY AND ARCHIVES CANADA CATALOGUING IN PUBLICATION

Singh, David, 1953-
Retire early and wealthy / David Singh.

ISBN 1-55022-751-3

1. Finance, Personal. 2. Retirement income — Planning.
I. Title.

HG179.S484 2006   332.024'014   C2006-902310-7

Cover design: Heather Taylor
Production: Mary Bowness
Printing: Transcontinental

This book is set in This book is set in Minion and Trajan

With the publication of *Retrire Early and Wealthy* ECW PRESS acknowledges the generous
financial support of the Government of Canada through the Book Publishing
Industry Development Program (BPIDP).

Canadá

DISTRIBUTION

CANADA: Jaguar Book Group, 100 Armstrong Ave., Georgetown, ON L7G 5S4

PRINTED AND BOUND IN CANADA

ECW PRESS
ecwpress.com

CONTENTS

STEP 1:
PROTECT YOUR FAMILY'S FUTURE WITH LOW-COST LIFE, DISABILITY AND CRITICAL CARE ILLNESS INSURANCE

STEP 2:
REDUCE YOUR TAXES AND CREATE MORE MONEY FOR INVESTMENTS AND A BETTER LIFESTYLE

STEP 3:
LEARN HOW TO INVEST SAFELY AND PROFITABLY   128

STEP 4:
LEARN HOW TO MANAGE YOUR DEBT!

STEP 5:
UNDERSTAND COMPOUND GROWTH

STEP 6:
USE THE POWER OF LEVERAGING TO CREATE LONG-TERM WEALTH

STEP 7:
UNDERSTAND THE POWER OF SYSTEMATIC WITHDRAWAL PLANS (SWP) AND LET THEM WORK FOR YOU

SOME FINAL THOUGHTS

Dedication

Every single day is an opportunity for me to do a little more than I did the day before; to learn a little more than I knew yesterday; and to dream a little more than I had previously.

My quest for KNOWLEDGE has been my biggest accomplishment in my life, and I encourage my readers to become life-long students of learning, as well. If you do, it will become your biggest, most precious asset — and your pathway to retiring earlier and wealthier than you ever imagined.

I dedicate this book to my children: Elesha (a brilliant university graduate who is infused with a passion to succeed), Shayna (a serious medical student who is determined to make a difference and save lives), Kendal (an undergraduate at Dalhousie University, who I know will find her own passion and success), and Julia (a 5-year-old who already has the courage to challenge her parents with her own ideas).

And to my friend Allan Gould, without whose encouragement, and brilliant editing, this book would not have been written.

INTRODUCTION

We are drowning in information but starved for knowledge.

— JOHN NAISBITT, AMERICAN AUTHOR OF
RE-INVENTING THE CORPORATION AND *MEGATRENDS*

Why is knowledge so important? That's like asking why breathing is important: without it, we cannot survive. Yet it is depressing, even shocking, how little **real knowledge** the vast majority of us possess about the things we care most about, and are even obsessed about, such as money, finances, debt, investments.

I often chuckle when I read that medical doctors who graduate from the world's top universities each year will have received less than *a few weeks of education* about **nutrition** over their decade or more of study. A creature from Mars — or even a teenager from Winnipeg! — might think to himself, "But *that* makes no sense! Every child knows that most diseases, from obesity to diabetes to heart, stomach or sleep problems, can be prevented by attention to diet!

Yet our physicians spend so *little time* in its study?"

The same can be said for MONEY. There is a very funny one-liner I've heard that goes like this: *"Money can't buy happiness; it can only buy the things that can MAKE you happy."* True, there must be tens of thousands of very wealthy men and women who are *not* happy with their lives, and for countless emotional and spiritual reasons. But there are *hundreds of millions* of others who are unhappy precisely because of their LACK of money: their towering debts, their fear of not making their next mortgage — or rent — payment, their endless worrying over how to replace their children's gym shoes or torn pants; their inability to put decent food on the table. (And there is nutrition, again!)

It is strange how little we all know about money, about finances, about stock markets, about taxes. If we taught our children as little about *cleanliness* as we do about money, welfare departments would take them away from us. But, that is the way we send them out into the world — and, indeed, that's the way most of our own parents sent US out into the world. (You should not be surprised to read that the vast majority of marital squabbles, and, yes, divorces, occur over financial matters, and NOT over children, religion, or sexual incompatibility. Money IS important. Just ask the next homeless person you see how he enjoys his life, if you don't believe me.)

I am hardly pleading innocence here. I, too, have risked money, wasted money, and, indeed, lost millions of my own, hard-earned dollars over the years. And this sad fact becomes ironic, when I note that I created, built up, and ran, for a decade, one of Canada's most successful financial planning companies, Fortune Financial, with over a thousand employees and some 700 financial planners, handling and investing some 10-billion-dollars of tens of thousands of my fellow citizens' precious assets. Yes, I did make a lot of money for many of these men and women, but in retrospect — I am now in my early 50s, starting several new businesses after many setbacks (you can read about my life in my recently published *A Passion to Succeed*) — *I could have done so much better* for most of my clients! Quite simply, I have more **knowledge** now.

I am not proud of the fact that I lost large sums of money in such scams as Bre-X, although it might seem almost shameful to admit this fact, having come from a family of 13 children on a subsistence farm in Guyana, in South America; you would *think* someone who had tasted, even lived in, severe poverty for the first two decades of his life would know better. But few of us "know better," and that is the point of this book: here we are, in the opening decade of the 21st century, continually flooded with information, yet lacking miserably in real knowledge, to paraphrase the inspired words of author Naisbitt, quoted at the opening of this Introduction. "GET YOUR MONEY INTO YOUR RRSP NOW!" we read one day; "THE HOT NEW STOCK (or MUTUAL FUND) IS X, Y, or Z" the next. The *so-called* experts speak hourly on this radio station or that TV station, and their words appear in dozens of newspaper and magazine articles every day, and so much of it is merely more "information," and *rarely* worthy of our attention. Sure, Google seemed overpriced when it first went public a few years ago, at 80 dollars U.S. a share, and millions must have kicked themselves when they saw it shoot up to $200, $300, $400 a share, even more, within two years. Those same millions, I'm sure, gleefully invested in hundreds of other high-tech funds in the crazed "stock market bubble" of the 1990s, and, while many did well, the vast majority lost nearly all of their investments, and even their pants, when the inevitable crash came in the spring of 2000. **Too much information, too little knowledge.** How stupid we are! *All* of us, including *this* author; this "financial expert."

Until recently, in my case. It has taken me over half my life to understand that, like riding a bike safely — one of the few skills our parents appear to have taught us well, in our childhoods — one must learn and understand THE RULES OF THE GAME. We must finally, finally — too often after years of wasted time, effort and money — discover how to MINIMIZE THE COST OF INSURANCE (while making sure that we buy the right kind, at the right age and right price); MINIMIZE THE AMOUNT OF INCOME TAXES WE PAY (and, yes, *legally* achieve this very-achievable goal); MAXIMIZE OUR INVESTMENTS (*risking* far less, *making* far more — and it's so *very, very easy!*), and other vital matters. Obviously, a little bit of research can help. Here, of course, we must be careful: the internet is like a giant, King-Kong-type library, run like an insane asylum. Sure, you'll get some valuable information, now-and-then, but it can be a real crap-shoot, as the gamblers say. As I've already noted, information is one thing; *true* knowledge is quite another. (I have a friend who bitterly told me, "type the word 'holocaust' into a search engine and you are just as liable to get lunatic neo-Nazis who deny that it ever took place, before you'll come across references to **The Diary of Anne Frank**." Sadly, the same goes for searching the World Wide Web for the best kind of insurance or the smartest investment concepts. In a way, we are all like a 10-year-old lonely kid who is sitting before a computer, looking for a friend; who knows if the person answering our requests is a predator?)

Here is a personal story, of which I am very proud: Exactly four years before I am writing these words — it was back in early 2002 — a good friend of mine, a retired police officer, asked me to manage his life savings for him. A half-dozen years earlier, I probably (and foolishly) would have plopped the $560,000 into a number of "actively-managed" mutual funds that I then had trust in, and hoped for a decent return. (Costing my friend up to 2.5%, even 3% of his profits in MER — Management Expense Ratios — to pay all those Smart Guys who are leaping in and out of dozens of stocks on each client's behalf, struggling to "time the market.")

Not in early 2002, not for any friend of mine; I had learned a lot over the years. What I did for this fine gentleman — and I've been doing for myself, over the same few years — was to invest every dollar of his in *five Index-Based Segregated Funds* (handled by TransAmerica Life Insurance), which simply follow the index (or indices) of various stock markets (such as the TSX (Toronto Stock Exchange) or the most famous, the Dow Jones (of the New York Stock Exchange). In other words, he now had his money in the top quality stocks which each index follows over the year. Boring? Sure. Not as thrilling as a penny stock which can double in a week and crash to nothing, a month later? No question.

What happened? As of early 2006, just four years after I acted on behalf of this fine ex-cop, the value of his investment had topped $900,000, for an *average annual rate of return of 15%* over that short period of time. Naturally, he is quite pleased, and is looking forward to a far less worrisome retirement with his spouse in the years ahead.

I would be negligent if I didn't mention something else: during those same four years — February 2002 to February 2006 — *nine out of ten of "actively-managed mutual funds" either lost money, or their performances averaged less than 5% per year.* As Bob Dylan slyly sang, four decades ago, "Something's happening, and you *don't* know what it is, DO you, Mr. Jones?"

Something *is* happening, good reader: some people, like myself, and, I hope, you, are waking up to the fact that "timing the market" rarely works. Sometimes it does, of course, and I would be hiding precious information from you if I denied that **fully 26 of Canadian Equity Mutual Funds** (that is, those who buy and sell — and buy and sell, and buy and sell — individual stocks of this country's companies — *did better* over the past year than I did, on behalf of my client, with my very unrisky investments, described above. Twenty-six! Good for them, and their bright, busy managers. There will always be some smart, crafty (and, I would say, lucky) men and women who do well with active trading — for a few months or a year or two. But there are **266** major Canadian Equity Funds, meaning that those 26 "active winners" represent *less than 10%* of these many "passively invested" mutual funds that "beat" the index. Now, if you knew that your chance of winning a million bucks in a lottery were nearly 1 in 10, you'd probably find that irresistible, and I couldn't blame you. But if I tell you that your chances of doing better, with purchasing an actively managed fund, than buying a very-low-risk, low-cost (that is, low MER) INDEX FUND, are **less** *than one-in-ten,* how many of you would bite?

Too many, alas. In 2005, there were some $23.4-BILLION poured into mutual funds sales in Canada, the best since 2001. Are we all crazy? Obviously, many millions of our citizens are, when I note that *the average return of the five largest Canadian Money Market Mutual Funds in 2005 was 1.5%!* (And $14.8 billion that same year was injected into those funds — ones that barely beat the inflation rate! They would have done nearly as well, stuffing their billions into their mattresses. (Or done better, merely depositing the billions into an ING Direct Savings Account, paying 2¾% that year, with no fee.) Oh, Mr. Jones, something IS happening, and has happened, in the world of investing — so why haven't more of us caught on to this vital, growing KNOWLEDGE?

I'm talking here mainly about ETFs, or Exchange Traded Funds, which are this simple, low-risk investment tool that reflects the performance of different sectors in the market, or broad indices of various stock markets — in Canada, the U.S., and world-wide. To be fair to me — and I want to be! — these wise investment vehicles were rare, when I was running Fortune Financial; today there are *hundreds* of them, with more being created every year. I will discuss these at great length in **Step 3**, below, but let me throw just a *few* facts (yes, knowledge) at you: in 2005, the value of ETFs that invested in the Canadian index shot up 28%; Brazil's ETFs zoomed 52% higher; and the ETF which followed the "Energy Sector" index in the United States increased in value by 34%. In a single year! So, how did YOUR portfolio do, during 2005?

All of us must keep this very important fact in mind: the Number One objective of every corporation is to maximize shareholder value; i.e., to maximize the rate of return that shareholders get on their investments in the shares of their corporation. Fair enough. Unfortunately, when it comes to maximizing shareholder value, *most times this is done at the expense of your savings, investments, and cost of insurance.*

What's the solution? *Knowledge, and not mere information.* The kind of knowledge that I hope to share with you in this book, which will give you at least a fighting chance to **win** at this Money Game, and help you RETIRE EARLY AND WEALTHY (to coin a phrase, and to echo the name of this book).

But it's no game, really; it is **life.** And as a famous line, variously attributed, goes, "I've been rich and I've been poor, and rich is better." I cannot guarantee you riches; no one can. (Although **I *am*** promised instant wealth in countless emails dumped into my computer, almost daily.) But I CAN promise you that you can do much, much better in your financial life, and, yes, retire earlier and better off than you ever dreamt possible, if you study the **money solution concepts** in the next section, and then, with my **7 Steps to Wisdom and Financial Freedom** that follow, you can achieve monetary peace of mind.

Good luck. Bob Dylan's "Mr. Jones" may not have known what's happening, but with more knowledge — filtered from the over-abundance of often lousy information that we are all drowning in — he, and all of us, can do *a lot better with our money,* and, by doing so, create a much less tense and more pleasurable future for ourselves, our loved ones, our descendants.

David Singh, Toronto
Spring 2006

SECTION
ONE

VALUABLE MONEY CONCEPTS AND SOLUTIONS FROM A TO Z

EARNING THROUGH LEARNING

The beginning of wisdom is to call things by their right names.

— CHINESE PROVERB

With this section, you are about to embark on a great journey. This journey is, of course, the Journey of Life, and our challenge is to make that life more satisfying, more comfortable, more rewarding. It is sad — tragic, really — how few of us ever learn about the importance of money, or about how it works. Not only do few parents teach their children this essential fact of life, as I noted in my Introduction, but our schools, as well, are notably and pathetically weak on this subject.

When you go on a trip, you know how important it is to take the time and effort to prepare: Did you remember to pack the cosmetics? Underwear? The dress shoes? The raincoat? The traveller's cheques? And most people, if they were planning to take a trip around the world, would know that their preparation should go beyond merely packing their suitcases. They would study the customs and the languages of the people they planned to encounter, and take along travel guides; they realize that otherwise, they would be totally lost. Yet when it comes to the ultimate Journey of Life, **the vast majority of us appear to be clueless about the most basic financial concepts.**

I want to help make your journey more pleasurable, more meaningful, and more rewarding in every sense of those words.

In this opening section, before we confront our **7 Steps,** I shall help you to understand the terminology — the jargon, or, as I think of them, the **valuable money solution concepts** — that you will run up against in this lifelong journey to knowledge, from A to Z. (Actually, from A to W — annuities to wraps.)

The following Money Solutions Concepts are discussed in this chapter:

- Annuities
- Asset Allocation
- Capital Gains
- Compound Interest
- Debt Management
- DPSPS — Deferred Profit-Sharing Plans
- Dividends
- Dollar-Cost Averaging
- Home Ownership and Mortgages
- Index Investing
- Inflation
- IPOS
- To Lease or Not to Lease
- Leveraging
- Limited Partnerships
- Market Timing
- Mutual Funds
- Offshore Investing
- Old Age Security
- Pension Plans
- RESPS — Registered Education Savings Plans
- RRIFS — Registered Retirement Income Funds
- RRSPS — Registered Retirement Savings Plans
- The Rule of 72
- Systematic Withdrawal Plans
- Wraps

ANNUITIES

An annuity is created when you turn your Registered Retirement Savings Plan (RRSP) over to a financial institution, usually an insurance company, on the important condition that you (or your spouse) will receive regular payments over a specified time period. The goal of this is, of course, to provide you with a guaranteed income, sometimes right up to the age of 90. The key to remember is, annuities can play an attractive role in converting assets you possess into a steady stream of income in your later years.

One of the best descriptions I've ever heard about annuities is, they are a kind of "reverse life insurance policy." Think about that image, because it will help you understand this often grotesquely complex concept: Most of us are aware that life insurance is based on the idea, "You send us payments regularly, and we'll pay you a lump sum when you leave this earth." Annuities, in almost mirror-like fashion, ask you to "Give us a lump sum, and we'll pay you regular payments over a specific period, possibly until your death — and possibly even after."

As most older Canadians know, RRSPs must be collapsed before the end of the year that their owners turn 69. That is when people may no longer make those exciting tax-free contributions. So now what? You certainly don't want to withdraw whole chunks of your RRSP, since the taxes would be devastating. There are two options open to you: to set up a Registered Retirement Income Fund (RRIF), or to create an annuity.

When you purchase an annuity with money out of your RRSP, *you don't have to pay any tax!* (The purchase is considered a tax-free "rollover" by the feds.) Naturally, those regular payments from the annuity will be taxed, in the same way as interest from a Guaranteed Investment Certificate (GIC) or savings account would be.

Questions and Facts About Annuities

The first question you must ask yourself if you are thinking about buying an annuity is this: How long do you want the payments to last? Some people choose a life annuity, which will keep the money coming until they die. Another possibility is a joint-life annuity, which will keep paying until both you and your spouse pass on. A third option is to pick the number of years you wish the annuity to run — say, 15, 10, or 5. When that time is up, the annuity will be gone, and the payments will stop.

Now, a real tough question: How much will that annuity pay you? This is decided by interest rates, since the insurance company is investing your money for you over this period, so be very careful which numbers you settle on. The difference a small interest-rate change makes in your payments over many years can be huge.

You'll also want to consider whether or not you want your annuity to be indexed, in which case it will be linked to inflation, so the payments will go up a bit each year. Consider, too, whether you want a guaranteed annuity, which will guarantee that the payments won't stop should you die, but would continue to go to your spouse or another beneficiary. Of course, these last two options are expensive, and if you choose them, the cost of your annuity will go up. Indexing and guarantees mean that the insurance company that sells you the annuity will probably be forced to pay out more money over a longer period of time, so they'll take more money off the top, and the payments you receive will be lower than for a "cheaper model."

Are there drawbacks to buying annuities?

Naturally. If you choose not to take out a guarantee, your loved ones won't see a penny after you die. Inflation can eat away at an annuity's value if you chose not to index it. And since the rate of return you will get from your annuity is fixed from the moment you buy it, you will lose the ability to take advantage of other possible investment options that may arise over the years; you give up control over your total savings, essentially. And you'll have to pay taxes on your annuity payments, as mentioned above.

But surely there must be advantages to annuities!
Of course. If you are not the type who loves to choose where to invest your money, but would rather have professionals do it for you, then annuities can put your mind at ease. Furthermore, with annuities, you know exactly how much you will have to live on in the years ahead. Annuities won't make you rich, though: if you buy one worth $50,000 that is guaranteed, say, for 15 years, you'd get payments that range between $4,000 to $5,400 annually, depending on the options you chose.

Annuities aren't "sexy" like ipos or high-tech stocks. But for hundreds of thousands of Canadians, they can prove to be, literally, a lifelong blessing

— and more than lifelong, if you choose the option that will continue payments for your beneficiaries!

Along with the RRIF, it's good to know that the annuity option is there for when you must finally collapse your RRSP. Just be aware: you must try to avoid paying too much for those attractive but costly extras, while not preventing easy access to the assets you've set aside for your anticipated retirement. The solution need not be daunting, at all. Consider investing only a portion of your retirement monies in one or two low-cost annuities (without any of those expensive options), and keeping the rest in a portfolio of stocks or mutual funds that you can reach for conveniently, when needed.

Money Solutions Annuities Highlights
- **Purchasing an annuity is one of two options — the other being an RRIF — available to you when you must collapse your RRSP at the age of 69.**
- **Annuities can guarantee that you and/or your spouse will receive regular payments over a certain period of time.**
- **Buying an annuity is considered a tax-free rollover from your RRSP. The actual annuity payments will be taxed like any other income.**
- **There are real advantages to purchasing an annuity, which are greater than any disadvantages. Just avoid putting all your retirement eggs in a single basket labeled "Annuity." How much you do put into annuities can depend on the amount of money you've put aside over the years, your life expectation, fears of shortfall, and more.**

ASSET ALLOCATION

It has been said by many experts that the key to investment success is diversification, a term usually defined as "spreading your investment risk by purchasing stocks and mutual funds in several different companies, industries, and even nations."

Fair enough. But *how* does one diversify effectively?

The answer is simple: through wise and patient **asset allocation**.

Asset allocation is usually interpreted as the distribution of one's investment assets, by percentage, into various different categories. You are *allocating* certain amounts of your assets to varieties of investment. So, you may put 35% of your money into equity mutual funds, 25% directly into stocks, 20% into precious metals, and 15% into real estate, keeping 5% in cash.

The mix you choose may change. For example, if you feel that the real estate market is heating up, you could choose to re-allocate all of what you had invested into precious metals into real estate, so that you end up with 35% of your total portfolio in that. Months later, you might decide that high-tech stocks are making a comeback, and re-allocate the 5% you still had in cash into stocks, as well as using more of the 30% you now have invested in stocks to buy shares in those kinds of companies.

And so on.

To prove the effectiveness — the sheer importance — of asset allocation, a landmark study was done several years ago, with the results published in the influential *Financial Analysts Journal*. By examining the performances of 82 large pension plans over a ten-year period, the research sought to explain why one institutional money manager makes more money than another.

The study found that 94% *of the difference in performance from one plan to another was a result of asset allocation, not investment selection!*

In other words, what truly matters is not *which* stocks you buy, but *what portion* of your total assets you place into stocks. So, the millions of investors who devote so much of their attention to trying to figure out what stocks to purchase are completely missing the point. **It's having money in stocks in the first place that is key.** With overwhelming evidence showing that most money managers/ stock brokers/financial advisors are *unable* to "pick the right stocks" or "know the right time to leap into the market," we must ask ourselves further questions: Why do these so-called experts continue to perform these proven-to-fail actions? Is it sheer stupidity? Greed? Pride? Or simply the triumph of hope over experience?

The good news is, there is an answer to all of this foolishness and futility: simply allocate your assets to various *index categories* (such as the Standard & Poor's 500, the TSX 300, the Dow Jones 30, a European index of major stocks, and so on), and you will be assured a much greater chance of success with your investments.

This is easy and efficient, and backed by reason and countless studies, all showing why **indexing should outperform** most "active" **money managers.** (By the latter, I mean the ones who are always buying and selling, trying to "time the market," building up huge tax costs from their endless purchases and sales, and forever leaping in and out of the marketplace like children at a wading pool.)

In **Step 3,** below, on Investment Planning, I will discuss in greater depth how you can design your own portfolio around this profound and powerful concept.

Money Solutions Asset Allocation Highlights
  • **Purchasing an annuity is one of two options — the other being an RRIF — available to you when you must collapse your RRSP at the age of 69.**
  • **Annuities can guarantee that you and/or your spouse will receive regular payments over a certain period of time.**
  • **Buying an annuity is considered a tax-free rollover from your RRSP. The actual annuity payments will be taxed like any other income.**
  • **There are real advantages to purchasing an annuity, which are greater than any disadvantages. Just avoid putting all your retirement eggs in a single basket labeled "Annuity." How much you do put into annuities can depend on the amount of money you've put aside over the years, your life expectation, fears of shortfall, and more.**

CAPITAL GAINS

The term "capital gains" does not refer to any extra money the President may have earned while living in Washington, D.C. (or the Canadian Prime Minister while living in Ottawa, for that matter). **Capital gains** refers to profits from the sale of an investment (stocks, bonds, real estate, units of mutual funds, etc.), *when you receive more than you paid for it.* Prior to February 27, 2000, the income inclusion rate for capital gains was 75%; on that date, it was reduced to 66 2/3%. (I'll discuss this in greater detail below, in **Step 2, on Tax Planning.**)

So, if you are on salary and are being hit by the highest income tax rate of around 50% (which means you are making over $60,000 annually), the capital gains tax on your successful investments would be approximately 33 ⅓%. That's still brutal, but it beats losing *one-half* to Ottawa, as you do with your regular earnings.

A Rare Tax Break from Our Federal Friends

There is one happy exception to having to pay capital gains tax on 75% of your "gains" from investments each year: when you sell your home. If you bought a house in Toronto in the early 1970s, before prices skyrocketed, for, say, $50,000, you may find that it is worth close to $1,000,000 in 2006. If you sell it, you have obviously made a profit of $950,000 — an impressive capital gain.

But a house is "forgiven" in the Canadian tax code, provided that it is your *principal residence.* If, that same year (or any other year), you sell a family cottage that you bought for $15,000 in 1960 but is worth, say, $200,000 today, *you will have to pay capital gains* on the increase of its value (less the money you put into it for improvements, etc.). You may have enjoyed the place every summer, but it was clearly not your main address over the years.

Whenever we purchase stocks, or mutual funds, or even Canada Savings Bonds, our goal is of course to "make money." Which means, if we are successful, that we will be hit regularly with taxes on capital gains dividends or interest. But there are ways to grow capital — to make capital gains — **more tax-efficiently.** A good accountant (or tax planning book) can help you reduce the size of that blow each year.

Here are a few tax-saving tips:

> • **Diversify and use wise timing to improve your tax-deferral possibilities.** For example, if you purchase Canada Savings Bonds, you are required by law to pay taxes on your earnings every single year — even though you won't have that money in hand until the bonds mature. Not too fair, but that's life (and a major flaw of savings bonds). But when you invest in assets that grow in value over a long period of time — your house, a portfolio of stocks, several mutual funds, etc. — you usually need *not* pay any capital gains tax until you finally sell the investment. Enjoy your wealth by using a systematic withdrawal plan, or SWP — see **Step 7** on this inspired strategy, later

in this book-and remember this key thought: if you don't sell, then capital gains tax is no tax!

• **"Spread the gains around" family members** (a.k.a. "income splitting"). When there are two or more members in a family earning income, they rarely make the same amount. The government's rules allow some capital gains to be listed as earnings of a spouse or dependent student, which can save you quite a bit of money.

• Invest inside such savings vehicles as RRSPS, RRIFS or, for the education of your children, RESPS, which allow money to grow in what is essentially a tax shelter. Indeed, an RRSP allows you to make good sums of money with excellent tax savings until you start to withdraw from it — often many decades after it was begun.

• **Remember how capital gains get taxed!** Never forget: A capital gain does not occur until an asset — cottage, stock, mutual fund, etc. — is *sold*, so any increases in the value of those assets are not taxable until then.

• **Make use of your capital losses.** You can offset capital gains that are taxable with capital losses, even from other years.

• **Purchase mutual funds early in the year.** Many mutual funds make a single, annual "capital gains distribution" to their shareholders each December, which can come in the form of cash, or as more shares. *Problem:* If you put money into a mutual fund late in the year, you'll get that nice little distribution all right, but you'll have to pay capital gains taxes to the same degree as someone who has held that fund all year! It's wiser, therefore, to make your mutual fund purchases early each year, or choose funds that make smaller distributions of profit. Better yet, invest in funds that make no distributions at all.

• **Avoid actively traded mutual funds.** There are some mutual funds that do *very little trading* — the buy-and-hold types. This approach cuts down on the amount of capital gains *they* make throughout the year, and, therefore, the amount of capital gains that you, as a shareholder, will be hit with, as well. Finally, don't forget that holding stocks and funds inside your RRSP, or a retirement plan sponsored by your employer, will make most of your capital gains distributions *not taxable* from year to year.

With thoughtful planning, capital gains taxes can be kept to a minimum.

Money Solutions Capital Gains Highlights
• Capital gains refers to the profits you make when you sell any investment for a greater amount than you paid for it.
• Capital gains are, happily, taxed at a lower inclusion rate than income.
• Gains on selling a home that is your principal residence do *not* get hit by capital gains taxes.
• There are several simple and legal ways to save on the taxes imposed on capital gains.

COMPOUND INTEREST

This is such a crucial financial concept, I am dedicating an entire section to it. **See Step 5, below.**

DEBT MANAGEMENT

This, as well, is one of the most vital of all financial concerns. **See Step 4,** which is entirely dedicated to this important aspect of monetary wisdom.

DPSPs — DEFERRED PROFIT-SHARING PLANS

A deferred profit-sharing plan, or DPSP, allows a company to share its profits on a tax-sheltered basis with employees who are not shareholders. DPSPs are a type of savings account that is based on the profits of the company you work for and paid into by your employer. Small companies are especially fond of these plans, because they can always save money during a lean period by eliminating (or decreasing) their contributions to the DPSP for that particular year.

What's especially attractive about DPSPs is that the money in them grows tax-free, allowing you, the employee, when you retire, to transfer what may eventually become a healthy sum into your RRSP, or to purchase an annuity. You are not allowed to put any of your own money into your DPSP; only your employer can contribute to it. The latter, in turn, gets a tax write-off for those contributions, so it's a win-win situation.

One of the most welcome aspects of DPSPs is that they are *not* as restricted as traditional RRSPs: you do not have to wait for a specific retirement age before you can withdraw any money. Naturally, as with an RRSP, you will have to pay income tax on any withdrawals you make from your DPSP, unless you transfer them directly into a company pension plan or your registered retirement plan.

A further advantage to DPSPs has to do with pension adjustments. These adjustments can be confusing, when you get involved in formulas where you subtract what you've been contributing to your personal RRSP. But the DPSP pension adjustment could not be easier: It's always the exact amount your employer has contributed to it over the past year.

As you can see, the DPSP is a helpful addition to your eventual retirement savings. The only catch, of course, is that you must build up your salary and years of service in order to get the most generous donations from your employer, and you must hope and pray that the firm you've chosen to work for makes a profit, at least most years you are with them.

Money Solutions DPSPs Highlights
• Think of DPSPs as a savings account provided by a profitable company to its employees.
• After years of growing tax-free, DPSPs can add a generous amount of money to your RRSP when you eventually retire.

DIVIDENDS

The American billionaire, John D. Rockefeller (1839-1937), once declared, "Do you know the only thing that gives me pleasure? It's to see my dividends coming in."

One can readily see why dividends brought old man Rockefeller such pleasure. They bring many a Canadian non-billionaire a lot of pleasure, too. Canadian companies often pay out dividends to those who have invested in them through purchasing their stocks or bonds. Of course, U.S. and other foreign corporations also pay dividends, but these are taxed at a much higher rate than those from our own country's businesses — a rare example of a real financial advantage to being a Canadian!

In the world of investment income, interest income is the most highly taxed of all, because it is fully included in your income, and taxed at your full marginal tax rate. Capital Gains, on the other hand, are the most tax-efficient. Indeed, only 50% of your capital gains income is included in your income, and taxed at your appropriate tax rate. In the very middle of the investment income spectrum, you'll find Canadian dividends. Those dividends from our home-and-native firms have always been tax- attractive, due to the dividend tax credit associated with them. Under the current rules, if you receive, say, $100 in dividends from a Canadian company, you "gross them up" by 25%, meaning that you actually report $125 of dividend income on your tax return. You are then entitled to claim a federal dividend tax credit equal to 13.3% of the crossed-up dividend, which can be used to reduce your federal tax payable! You are also entitled to a provincial tax credit, based on the tax rate of each province in our country.

The following, simple example shows how a top-bracket taxpayer is taxed on a $1,000 dividend that was received in 2005; this should clarify any questions which may have arisen to this point:

TAXATION OF $1,000 AT THE HIGHEST MARGINAL TAX RATE (IN ONTARIO)

Cash Dividend: $1,000   Gross up: $250   Total: $1,250

Federal Tax of 29%	$363.
Dividend Tax Credit	($166).
leaving you	$197.
Provincial Tax (8.96%), takes away	$112.
Total Tax on your Cash Dividend of $1,000:	$309.
Amount retained by you after tax on that $1,000 dividend:	$691.

Let's look at the different amounts of taxes payable on $1,000 of Interest, and Capital Gains Income, compared with Dividends, for that Ontario Resident in the highest marginal tax rate: On Interest, the hit would be $464, which is a brutal tax rate of 46.4%; on Capital Gains, it would be the far lighter $232 (which is, of course, 23.2%); and you already saw the rate on Dividends: $309, or 30.9%.

Since dividends are paid out of a company's after-tax profits, our beloved friends in Ottawa recognized that it would be unfair to tax the same profits twice — first at the source, and then again later, when you get the dividend cheque. So our partners in Ottawa cleverly figured out that dividend tax credit. It's complicated, I can assure you, but the bottom line is that it allows those lovable dividends to be taxed at a lower rate than your salary and other earnings.

While the pleasure that dividends can bring you may be undercut a bit by having to pay tax on them at all, at least those taxes can be reduced somewhat, due to the tax-friendly attitude of the feds toward dividends that flow from Canadian businesses.

It makes sense, really: Why not tax dividends from foreign businesses fully, at the same marginal tax rate that applies to your regular earnings? It might encourage our citizens to lean toward investing in our own country's companies. Call it chauvinism if you will, but what country in the world is not eager to support and encourage its own businesses?

If you receive dividends from Canadian stocks, you will also receive T3 or T5 slips, or a T5013, depending on the source of the dividends. These forms will ensure that you get the full dividend tax credit to which you are entitled for buying Canadian. Dividend earnings can also often be transferred from a higher-earning to a lower-earning spouse, to help you cut your taxes even further.

Dividends can be an important part of your annual earnings — although let us hope that they are not the only pleasure you get in life, like "poor" Mr. Rockefeller!

Money Solutions Dividends Highlights
 • **Dividend tax credits from Ottawa mean that dividends are taxed at a lower rate than salary earnings.**
 • **Buying Canadian investments guarantees this welcome tax break.**

DOLLAR-COST AVERAGING

We tend to laugh at the value of our dollar as compared to the mighty Yankee buck, over most of the past few decades (especially now that our dollar comes in coin form). But we should respect the remarkably helpful investment concept called dollar-cost averaging; it's one that every wise person should attempt — no, vow — to use.

As one financial author puts it, "Dollar cost averaging is the greatest tool at an investor's disposal for a long-term investment program. The concept of dollar cost averaging suggests that the best way to invest is by a systematic program of equal amounts over a reasonable period of time, particularly for RRSPs and RESPs, which require a periodic, long-term asset accumulation plan." I could not agree more, although I would *not* limit its use only to RRSPs.

A cynic might call dollar-cost averaging a "forced savings plan" or "the best way to shame you into putting money away on a regular basis," and these statements wouldn't be far from the truth. To take advantage of dollar-cost averaging, you *simply invest a certain amount of money at certain intervals of time.* This might be $25 a week, $50 on the first day of every month, $1,000 — or $5,000, if you can afford it — every quarter. **The key is to do it.** Never forget: it's not about *how much* you invest; it's about *how consistently* you invest.

Okay, you might think, I get the **dollar** idea, but what's the **averaging?**

Well, if the $100 every month that you plow into an equity mutual fund buys you 10 shares of that fund on March 1 of one year because the fund is valued at $10 on that particular day; and, on April 1, your next $100 investment will buy only 9 shares because the fund has increased to over $11 during that brief period, you have "averaged out" the expense of your purchase. You now own 19 shares, and you *don't* get all carried away muttering to yourself, "The shares were so much cheaper back in early March! Why didn't I buy more then?" — the kind of attitude that can be fatal to successful investing. Dollar-cost averaging captures perfectly the moral of Aesop's fable of the tortoise and the hare: **Slow and steady will always win the race,** even if there are upsetting moments and frightening detours along the way.

What Else Is Great About Dollar-Cost Averaging?

By now you should have an idea of my opinion of market timing. Here is where you learn *one of the most positive aspects of dollar-cost averaging:* it takes the scary notion of "knowing **when** to invest" out of the act of investing. After all, if you are always putting in that $50 a week (or whatever), you can't — or at least shouldn't — get obsessed with the daily machinations and zigzags of stock and mutual fund prices, which we should all be ignoring, anyway.

As I shall discuss again elsewhere in this book, *fear* is a real problem for most investors. Will the stock fall further? Should I wait till the bear market runs its course before climbing back in? Is the stock too high for me to get on board now? (As if *anyone* can *ever* know the perfect day or time to "jump in.") But with your money steadily going into your investment account, averaging out the "dollar cost" over the long haul, **you really can't lose.** You are continually, inexorably, slowly but surely purchasing more and more shares, and the cost of those you bought at $13, at $17, and at $19 (or at $6, for that matter) will average out over the years and decades.

Indeed, as many experts have pointed out, since you are constantly building up a larger and larger number of shares in your portfolio, you have **ensured** through dollar-cost averaging that *you have bought the largest number of those shares when the price was low, and the fewest when the price was high.* (Think about it for a moment: When the stock or fund was at $5, you were managing to purchase 20 of them for your monthly $100 investment; if it has now hit $20, you are only buying five, are you not? So you're buying far fewer at the much higher price!) Stock markets inevitably go up and down, up and down; it's the way they work. Dollar-cost averaging helps remove that almost inevitable worry (and panic) that hits nearly every investor with each nerve-wracking zig and zag of the TSE, Dow, S&P, and Nasdaq. If we measured the height of our young children every single day, we might well get all concerned over them "not growing."

Many financial advisors have laughingly noted that dollar-cost averaging can be most attractive of all when the fund or stocks you choose to invest in are all over the map, like a Mexican jumping bean. By **always** investing the same amount of money every single week or month, wild fluctuations in the market allow you to keep buying that stock or fund cheaply, when the *fearful* investors are dumping their shares and running for the hills. In other words, *you find yourself often getting your investments at deep discount prices!*

Is There Any Downside to Dollar-Cost Averaging?
Yes, but only if you fail to keep your emotions in check, and leave your chequebook in chaos. If you have sudden expenses (family illness, loss of job, etc.), you may fail to keep your promise to invest that small/large amount every single month. *Stay the course.* Set aside that weekly or monthly or quarterly amount, and start dollar-cost averaging. You'll thank me, and so will your spouse, children, and inevitably wealthy descendants.

Money Solutions Dollar-Cost Averaging Highlights
• Dollar-cost averaging is a systematic program of investing equal amounts of money over (preferably long) periods of time.
• This wise approach to "forced savings" cuts down on the fear-producing effect of the typical, universal, and inevitable ups and downs of the world's stock markets.
• For dollar-cost averaging to work, you must be consistent in your weekly or monthly investment, regardless of emotions and monetary tensions.

HOME OWNERSHIP AND MORTGAGES

Home is where the money is, along with the heart. Home ownership has long been a major part of the Canadian (and American) Dream. And even though we are forever being reminded that "a house is the most expensive purchase we will ever make," the desire to settle down, to stop paying rent, and to own those walls that you hammer your nails into and hang your pictures on, is a deeply felt, almost universal one.

Is It Wise to Actually Purchase a Home, and Put Out All That Money?
Buying a house in 2006 is hardly the guarantee of wealth that it was in the

early 1970s, when house prices were doubling nearly every year, reaching grotesque peaks in the late 1980s, then crashing; only since the mid-90s have they been moving up steadily again. Still, the argument for home ownership remains strong, and for several reasons.

For one, you need only give a downpayment; you never have to pay the full price of a house (whether its $95,000, $250,000 or $870,000), since purchasers can always leverage (**see Step 6, dedicated to Leveraging, below**) the cost through taking out a mortgage. Normally, you can put down as little as 25% of a house price, and mortgage/leverage the rest. So, a $300,000 house would demand a downpayment of "only" $75,000. But even here, there are exceptions and attractive alternatives.

For instance, there is an option called "high-ratio" mortgage, which allows many potential purchasers in this country to put down only 10% of the price of a house, and borrow the remaining 90%. And the Canada Mortgage and Housing Corporation (CMHC) has a tempting program that allows many first-time home buyers to shell out as little as 5% of the purchase price (that's *only $10,000* on a $200,000 house or condo)!

Then, there is the option of borrowing up to $20,000 from your RRSP for the purpose of buying a home (a husband and wife buying a home together can borrow this amount each from their respective RRSPs). This money has to be repaid into the plan over the following 15 years, and since this repaying is, naturally, not considered a new contribution to the RRSP, it is not tax-deductible. Still, it is a pleasant option, and one worth checking into at your bank or nearest tax office.

Another good reason to purchase a home has to do with the wonderful "gift" from the feds in Ottawa that I discussed under **capital gains,** above. Your principal residence will probably (but not necessarily) show impressive capital gains over the years of ownership, but *those gains will be tax-free.*

So, say that your home appreciates (i.e., increases in value) by 10% over the next few years, from $300,000 to $330,000 — hardly an impossibility in a major Canadian city. That entire 10% — that $30,000 — would be tax-free. Imagine such government largesse if you made 10% on a stock or mutual fund sale! Indeed, you would probably have to clear up to 20% on any (necessarily taxed) investment to match the same profit you would earn from the appreciation of the value of your home.

Then There's That Mortgage — What to Do with It?

Whether your mortgage is for 75% of a house's purchase price or 95%, the fact remains that anyone who buys a home is going to be seriously in debt, and for a good many years. (It's not by chance that the word "mortgage" comes from the Old French, and means "death pledge.")

There are many kinds of mortgages — amortized, convertible, open, short- or long-term, fixed- or variable-rates — and these are all worth looking into. After all, if you believe that interest rates are going to go up, then as a wise new homeowner you would definitely want to lock in today's (low) rates for several years. And if you feel sure that interest rates are likely to fall, then mortgages with extremely short terms (one year, even six months) are the most sensible.

Which leads us to one of the most troublesome and problematic questions that all homeowners, whether new or old, must face: *should one pay off that "death pledge" as quickly as possible?* Financial experts are by no means in agreement on this one.

Mortgages on houses can end up costing homeowners many tens of thousands of dollars over the original purchase price; in many cases, one will pay over twice the price of the home, spread over the many years of the mortgage. "Pay off your home mortgage!" is the crystal-clear advice of the respected author Henry B. Zimmer, whose *Canadian Tax and Investment Guide* is a perennial bestseller. "If you are typical of most Canadians" he writes, "the first major step in proper planning is to discharge your home mortgage as quickly as possible. . . . The only exception might be if you are one of the very few people with a low-interest 'locked-in' mortgage that dates back to the pre-inflation era."

But not everyone agrees with Mr. Zimmer. Some financial planners see mortgage payments as a kind of "regular forced savings plan," pointing out that, over time, you'll gradually pay down your home loan and increase your equity.

The money manager who impressed me most on this issue is Ric Edelman, whose delightful 1998 book *The Truth About Money* often takes the contrarian point of view. Indeed, the author dares to give "Five great reasons to carry a big long mortgage"! I shall summarize his reasoning, here:

First, home values are not touched by the size of mortgages, and the vast majority of houses will go up in price over the years, regardless. So why pour money into the place when you could spend it or grow it better else-where? Second, in a world where car loans can run 8 to 10% and credit cards 18% to 26% and beyond, mortgages on houses are far cheaper, and far closer to the prime rate. And — if you borrow against your home, using the ever-increasing value of the house as your collateral — you can deduct the interest of that loan when you use the money to invest — just like your American relatives have been allowed to do on *their* mortgage payments for many decades. So Edelman argues, "get a big mortgage, enabling you to use your cash to pay off other [usually far more costly] debts." In this case, I concur with his contrarian view.

His other reasons are less persuasive, but I'll just give you his conclu-sion, based on the "first academic study undertaken on the question of 15-year vs. 30-year mortgages," in the April 1998 issue of *The Journal of Financial Planning*, which is published by the Institute of Certified Finan-cial Planners in the United States. Their conclusion may be surprising to you: "The 30-year loan is best." The long-term mortgage has many interest-ing advantages, but the key ones, we suggest, are that your cash will always be available to you if you need it for emergencies, because the mortgage payment remains fixed while your income will probably grow due to infla-tion and your increased experience; ultimately, you'll be paying off a loan fixed long ago, with what will eventually be *far less valuable* future dollars.

There's no doubt, however, that home ownership can be scary, and that it is one of the most important decisions — and inarguably the most expen-sive — that you and your partner will ever make.

Money Solutions Home Ownership and Mortgages Highlights
• There are several ways to purchase a home that need not demand a large down-payment.
• A primary residence is always free of capital gains taxes; since the vast majority of houses increase in value, house buying is nearly always a wise move.
• There are strong arguments for carrying a large and lengthy mortgage, including the use of one's home for collateral in borrowing money to invest. This allows you to deduct the interest on that loan, which means that you are essentially writing off mortgage costs, which is what Americans have always done.

INDEX INVESTING

This brilliant type of "passive" investing will be covered at length in **Step 3**, below, on **Investing Safely and Profitably.**

INFLATION

Inflation. The comedians love to joke about it (one once declared, decades ago, "There are plenty of good five-cent cigars in the country. The trouble is, they cost a quarter"), but if you plan to live beyond the age of 50 — make that 30 — then to ignore it is like ignoring a hungry grizzly bear or lion in your living room.

The metaphors are endless, but then, so is inflation. This dreadful, universal problem truly demands far more frightening images than lions, killers or even icebergs; perhaps an MRI of a slow-growing cancer best captures its destructive potential, since inflation *is* a silent but inexorable killer — and one not easily slowed, much less stopped. Since inflation is so frighteningly dangerous over several years, it's amazing how many of us ignore it entirely.

Slashing the Value of Everything

Over the last few years of the 1990s and right into the second half of the first decade of the 21st Century, North Americans had it *easy,* with annual inflation rates at 40-year lows — 2.5% and less. But even those low numbers can add up as well, over a period of time. Just think of your investment returns: If you made 8% on a bond or mutual fund in a recent year, and paid taxes of 3.2% (assuming a 40% marginal tax rate), you were left with 4.8%. Take away the average inflation over the past decade — 2.2% — and *your net earnings were actually only 2.6%.*

But these past few years were utterly atypical of the past several decades, and must not blind us to the destructive power of this most cruel of economic facts of life. In the last quarter century, the annual rate of inflation in North America has often been as brutal as a tyrannosaurus rex running wild in Jurassic Park: 8.9% in 1981; 12.4% in 1980; 13.3% in 1979; 12.2% in 1974; 8.8% in 1973 . . . Oh, yes; the last time there was a *decline* in the cost of living in our Home and Native Land was over a half-century ago — in 1953. In that year, and in that year only, your dollars were actually capable of purchasing *more* at your local store than the year before. But *not once* since then has such a **deflation** occurred!

Many Canadians have trouble planning for next week, much less next year (or for their unimaginably far away retirement, for that matter). This lack of foresight can have tragic consequences for their future financial health. Imagine, for a moment, a 50-year-old woman earning $50,000 a year today. She wants to retire in 15 years, with the same lifestyle and the same income. There's bad news for Ms. Rose H. Canadian: Since inflation has averaged approximately 5.5% every year since the early 1970s until only recently, her $50,000 of the year 2006 will have only a *fraction* of today's buying power in the year 2021. Indeed, she conceivably will need close to $120,000 from her pensions, stock dividends, oas, rrsp, etc. to keep living the way she does today, and she had better have a net worth of *over $2 million* in order to sustain the comfortable life she had back in 2006.

No Escape

Inflation, like air pollution and global warming, is all around us. And it is potentially just as deadly. There is no "solution" to inflation. The closest we as a society can get to slowing down (but not curing) this cancer eating away at our savings, our investments, our profits, our compound interest, the value of our money, and any hopes of a decent retirement, is to ensure that the heads of the Federal Reserve in the United States and the Bank of Canada keep a watchful eye on the bank rates, and on inflation itself. What we *can* do — each of us — is to keep inflation in mind, just as we listen to the weatherperson warning us against strong ultraviolet rays of the sun during certain summer days. Inflation will rarely hit the stratospheric 8 to 12% levels of the 1970s and 1980s — we pray! — but it will always be there, eating away at our purchasing power, like a termite in wood.

Inflation is a silent killer. Keep its deadly effect in your consciousness whenever you plan for your future, when you figure out your compound interest and investment earnings, and when you ask yourself, "how much money will I need to live like I am now, in 10, 20, or 30 years?" If you do that, you will do a *lot* better in your later years, and be able to enjoy them more.

Money Solutions Inflation Highlights

• Inflation is no laughing matter; rather, it is a cancer that eats away at all investments and future financial stability and happiness.

• Rates of return — so crucial to monetary success — are often decimated by inflation. Inflation must be factored into any expectations you have for your portfolio — even when it is as low as it has been over the past decade.

IPOs

"IPO." Those are initials that your parents and grandparents probably saw and heard a lot less often than other ones, such as RCMP or FBI.

But this acronym — which stands for **initial public offering** — was seen everywhere over the last dozen years. In the booming 1990s, it seemed like millions and even billions of dollars were being made every other day, as more and more technology-based firms "went public" on the Nasdaq exchange in New York. And when we hear that $10,000 (U.S.) invested in the IPO of the popular website Yahoo! in 1997 was worth over *$1.5 million* in early 2000 — barely three years later! — millions of investors were following high-techs and seeing visions of Dawson City and the Klondike. **There must be enough gold for everybody!**

Not So Fast, Smart Investor; Not So Fast
First of all, an important fact: IPOs do have great value, at least potentially, to the companies that offer them. After all, selling shares to the public for the very first time helps small and promising firms to obtain capital — the money they need to build their companies by purchasing other businesses, adding staff, paying down debt, increasing advertising and creating brand awareness, etc. Quite simply, capital allows a firm to grow. In other words, IPOs are no scam. They are a legitimate, even essential, way for young businesses to expand and possible prosper.

But *can the average, small investor "get in" at the offering price of an IPO* which interests them? Alas, don't hold your breath, dear John and Jane Canadian. When a bank "underwrites" an IPO, it always wants to reward its best institutional investors with the possible windfall. Naturally, retail brokerage houses see an IPO as a reward for their very best brokers. And those brokers, in turn, will want to reward their very best clients. And by *best,* we mean *wealthiest.*

And if it's an *American* IPO — as 98% of the hot, high-tech companies on Nasdaq in recent years have been — it's *utterly impossible for you to get in early.* This is because, under Canadian law, unless the prospectus of a young, going-public company has been filed in our country, it is simply not legal for anyone above the 49th parallel to buy into the offering at the opening, or "deal," price.

Consider this rather sobering example: When the very popular high-tech company Palm went public on Nasdaq not that long ago, the deal price was $32 U.S. But by the first moment *any* Canadian had a chance to purchase that very hot stock, it cost over $160 a share — five times its original price!

There is a further problem. Asking most analysts about an IPO with which their brokerage house is involved is like asking a new mother if her new-born baby is beautiful. *Of course* the kid is gorgeous. (Brilliant, too). Research has shown that in most sales of IPOs by brokers to their "favourite clients," the brokers are paid *double* what they would make on a traditional stock transaction!

Furthermore, IPOs often involve "holding periods," so you can't quickly sell that thrilling high-tech stock as it doubles, triples, and quadruples in price (as so many did in the Nasdaq nineties, until that market began to tank, horrifically, if predictably, in April of 2000). If you do choose to dump your IPO shares early, you'll actually be penalized from participating in future IPOs that your broker may be involved in. To quote one Wall Street leader, "the IPO process is all about greed."

Markets are crazy. They are all on Valium one day, and on amphetamines (speed) the next. We all know that, even if we too often forget it. Look at how gold shot from $35 an ounce in the late 1960s way up to over $800 a dozen years later, then crashed miserably; it staggered around the $300 level for fully two decades, until a healthy run-up after 2003. A handful of men and women got rich, sure. But 95% lost their shirts (or blouses). Need we mention Bre-X or LivEnt, Enron or WorldCom?

An Expert Weighs In

Here are some excerpts from an interesting article written by Rohen Farzad for Dow Jones, and reprinted in Canada's *Financial Post* on December 9, 2000, under the headline "How the Street rips off investors on tempting IPOS":

> *Every small investor dreams of getting in on an initial public offering (IPO). Fast gains, easy money, better same day returns than a Tony Soprano rendezvous with an armoured truck. Or so the mythology goes. Most investors have never heard of an insidious little practice known as the syndicate penalty bid, whereby an underwriting firm revokes a broker's commission should his client sell his IPO shares too quickly. The penalty bid presents a big disincentive for brokers to tell their clients to get out of an IPO even when it's clear the company is a dog. The result: after insiders and preferred institutional clients cash out, retail investors are usually left holding the bag. . . . With few exceptions, those who wish to play the high stakes IPO game at the retail level must submit to their broker's expectation that they pony up for pretty much every deal a particular bank brings to market — from hot IPOs to postponed cold issues, secondary offerings to convertible deals. This is a losing quid pro quo: For every oversubscribed IPO that triples or quadruples in its first day of trading, the kind of deal that offers the poorest share allotments, the client must also swallow several issues that are destined to languish in the penalty-bid dog house.*

Now, which would *you* rather put your money into? Quality, proven equities? Mutual fund companies which invest in excellent stocks, or, much better, ETFs which invest in entire sectors, even whole countries? Or the initial public offerings of fledgling companies, of which eight or nine collapse or fail for every single one which succeeds?

I think you know the answer. Buying lottery tickets or flying to Vegas may give you better odds.

Money Solutions IPOs Highlights
- IPOs (initial public offerings) are valuable to start-up companies in that they help them to raise money on the stock market. But they are *rarely* good investment opportunities.
- IPO, like lotteries, are about greed, not about wise investing. Even "insiders" lose money on IPO, up to nine times out of ten.
- Things are even worse for *Canadians* trying to make fast profits with U.S. offerings; by law, Canadians cannot buy directly into a U.S. IPO.
- It is dangerous for investors to look to analysts for objective opinions about a company.
- Wall Street (and Bay Street) research has become almost worthless and I don't think the average investor can benefit from it, given all the bias. My best advice is: *Do your own research!*
- With most IPOs, brokers are paid double what they would make on a regular stock transaction.
- Before participating in an IPO, ask your broker what the holding period is, and whether you will be penalized from participating in future IPOs if you sell the stock prior to the end of the holding period. Write down his response.

TO LEASE OR NOT TO LEASE

Buying a car will probably be one of the major expenditures of your adult life, surpassed only by the purchase of a house. The fact that most cars cost upwards of $25,000 nowadays may move a lot of us to think a little about how to approach this costly but very necessary item in our lives. This leads us to a question few of us ask: *Should you buy a new car the next time you need one, or should you lease it?* Let us eliminate, right off the bat, those who should not even *consider* the concept of leasing. Ask yourself the following questions:

1. **How long do you tend to keep your car before looking for a new one?** Are you like many "old-fashioned" types (such as, perhaps, your parents?) who love to drive a vehicle until its fenders fall off, or its repairs become prohibitively expensive?
2. **Do you pile the miles on each year?** Most leases provide a

penalty for anyone who drives over 24,000 km (15,000 miles) a year, or 100,000 km (60,000 miles) over a four-year term. The penalty can be pretty stiff — up to 25 cents a mile.

If you answered yes to either of these questions, then don't even *think* about leasing a car. Leasing works best for people who put low mileage on their cars for under four years, at which time they are ready and eager to hand it back to the leasing firm and choose a new one. Those who love to drive a car until its bumpers and wheels break off, or who drive long distances daily to and from, or during, work, would be wasting their time looking into leasing.

Those Who Drive for Business
On the other hand, if you are in some kind of business in which you need to drive, and *should* have a handsome new car every few years to look more impressive for your clients — and are deducting most of your costs as business expenses — then leasing could well be the way to go.

As most people in business know, taking tax deductions — whether for that fax machine at home or for entertaining clients at fancy restaurants and with theatre tickets — is an important part of tax planning. Indeed, when it comes to the wonderful world of business, even the number of miles you drive should not prevent you from leasing, because you can always deduct those extra charges, as well.

Even the most anti-leasing, "never-lease-cars!" investment planners admit that leasing makes sense to the business person who deducts driving costs as one more expense on their tax return.

How About the Rest of Us?
Many financial writers are as down on leasing cars as much as they are on playing with penny stocks or day trading. "Leasing is . . . generally a bad financial move," write the bright guys who pen *Personal Finance for Dummies for Canadians*. "[L]easing is even more expensive than buying a car on credit. Neither is a good option. Save and pay cash. Buy what you can afford."

That may have some good advice in it, but how many of us can afford to not use credit to purchase a car? And how many of us ever manage to be able to "save and pay cash"?

And so, a growing number of men and women — and not only businesspeople — look at leasing a car. Leasing can be attractive to many because, to be blunt, you don't really *own* the thing; you're *renting* it. Like a rented car, you can forget about the responsibilities of ownership — you don't worry about maintaining equity. Since you return the car at the end of the term lease, your monthly (lease) payments are naturally less than what a car loan would be, because you pay only for the interest and the car's depreciation.

One of the real advantages — if not pleasures — of leasing a car, has to do with the smaller amount of that money you must shell out each month. Two simple examples will suffice:

> *Charlie wants to buy a car that costs around $35,000. He must hand over one-fifth as a downpayment, and take out a four-year loan from the bank (or car dealership), which will run approximately 7%. The 20% down will cost Charlie $7,000, and his monthly payments will run just over $650 a month.*

> *Joyce, on the other hand, chooses to **lease** the exact same car, which means that she will not have to pluck seven grand from out of her stock portfolio that has been doing so well. After paying the necessary one-month (refundable) security deposit, her monthly payments will be some $200 less than Charlie has to pay to own the car.*

As you can see, Joyce will have around $2,500 more disposable money, every year, to play with or invest, than Charlie will — not to mention the downpayment Charlie paid that she did not.

So why do many car dealers love to lease, when they will be getting several hundred dollars less each month over a three- or four-year period? For one thing, they get the car back at the end of the term, so they'll be able to sell it a second time!

Smart Leasing Strategies

It's easy to lose all the great advantages of leasing by ignoring a few key aspects of the deal. For instance, avoid paying for costly extras — unnecessarily glamorous trims and ritzy leather interiors, mini-disc players, or anything along those lines. After all, the car isn't yours, so why pay extra for several options that you'll be giving up at the end of your term?

Then, there are the capitalized cost reductions. Dealers love to push potential leasing customers into paying this, letting them lower their payments. *Don't do it*. Instead, request that you make additional "security deposits." You'll get those deposits back at the end of the leasing term, without having to shell out so much in capitalized cost reductions.

Finally, it is essential — crucial! — that you have "gap insurance." This covers the "gap" between a car's residual value — what it is worth at the end of the lease term according to the lease contract — and what it's actually worth. If you have an accident during the lifetime of your lease, then you may well find that you'll have to pay thousands of dollars, which your insurance company will refuse to pay, because a "gap" exists between what each side claims the car is now worth. Be careful!

Be sure to read the fine print. As the major 7 **Steps** in this book that follow this section will show you, there's a lot that you can do with that hefty downpayment that you (unlike Charlie) will save. Just imagine how much $7,000 could grow over a few years, in an excellent stock or mutual fund portfolio!

We believe that, in general, ***ownership is far better than lending*** — for example, we recommend purchasing stocks (which you own) over bonds (which involve lending money to a company or government).

But when it comes to a car, we think leasing *is* worth some serious thought. Several money experts put it this way: "Rent what depreciates; buy only what appreciates." Houses, of course, are in the latter category; cars, on the other hand, depreciate from the moment you first turn the key in the ignition — often $10,000 or more on the first day. For the right kind of driver, there can be some definite advantages to a car lease.

Leasing Language 101
To make your life a little easier, here are some important leasing terms. You may find the following definitions helpful if you decide to pursue the idea of leasing a car for yourself or your business:

- **cap cost reduction** — a downpayment;
- **net capitalized cost** — the basis for figuring lease payments, including the vehicle, accessories, optional services, and the deduction of any cap cost reduction;

• **closed-end lease** — a lease in which the lessor assumes all residual risks;

• **depreciation** — a reduction in the vehicle value over a period of time;

• **early termination** — the terminating of a lease before its scheduled end;

• **excess mileage charge** — the charge per mile made for the number driven over the maximum amount specified in the lease;

• **lessee** — the user of the vehicle who signs the lease and is responsible for compliance with it;

• **lessor** — the owner of the leased vehicle — i.e., the car dealership;

• **open-end lease** — a lease under which the lessee guarantees the residual value of the vehicle;

• **residual value** — the lessor's original estimate of the vehicle's value at the scheduled end of the lease; and

• **security deposit** — a refundable amount that is used to cover customer amounts that are owed, but not paid, at the end of a lease.

Money Solutions Leasing Highlights

• Leasing a car should at least be *considered* by intelligent people — unless they tend to drive cars till they fall apart, or load up too many miles on them.

• Leasing is especially attractive to those who must drive as part of their work, and deduct expenses.

• There are easy things one can do to keep leasing costs down.

• "Gap insurance" is a must, should you choose to lease.

• Leasing a car could very well free up money for thoughtful investing.

LEVERAGING

This is another one of those essential terms, and financial concepts, which deserve an entire portion of a book of their own; **see Step 6 on The Power of Leveraging,** below.

LIMITED PARTNERSHIPS

Limited partnerships are reminiscent of another use of the initials LP: the long-playing record. Both things are outmoded pleasures — things of the past, scratched and damaged. Neither has much value today.

Limited partnerships invest in a variety of businesses: usually real estate, but also mining, gas and oil exploration, and even the production of TV shows and movies. A limited partner (unlike a general partner) cannot incur obligations on behalf of the partnership, and need not participate in day-to-day management or operations of the business. In the vast majority of cases, the role of the limited partner is to invest money in a company, or any other project, in exchange for a share of the (possible) profits it generates. It's great not to have any liability beyond one's own monetary contribution toward a business, and for many years, tens of thousands of Canadians participated in limited partnerships.

Today, however, we find it informative that if you look up "limited partnership" in the bestselling annual tax guide *Evelyn Jacks on Tax Savings,* you are directed to a section entitled "Limited Partnership Losses of Other Years." In fact, "losses" is *usually* the key word attached to the term "limited partnerships."

If the above is true, then why on earth were limited partnerships so popular for so many years?

LPS were extremely popular — if not successful — precisely because there were numerous tax loopholes — most of them now closed by our ever-vigilant, money-hungry federal government — that allowed many Canadians to hope to see their various limited partnerships grow by up to 20% a year, and to receive generous dividends of close to 10%. This rosy picture had a fat chance of actually materializing — but then, the partner could always write off the losses and save some taxes; see Evelyn Jacks' book for more on the subject.

Money Solutions Limited Partnerships Highlights
 • Limited partnerships can be successful, but more often than not, they turn out badly for many that get involved.
 • Limited partnerships have obvious advantages, in that financial obligations are limited, and daily participation in the "deal" is not necessary.

• Most tax loopholes that once made limited partnerships attractive have been eliminated over the years by the federal government, but there are still ways to use limited partnerships to reduce your taxes and invest wisely at the same time.

MARKET TIMING

Market timing is like "live recording," "military intelligence," "airplane food" or "jumbo shrimp" — a phrase consisting of two words that simply do not go together in any sensible way; in other words, an oxymoron. Those who time the market follow "technical analysis based on price trends for individual stocks or the market as a whole. Really good market timers are a rare breed and very hard to find," to quote one financial writer. *Impossible* to find, I suggest, after spending over a quarter century in the investment business.

It Just Doesn't Work

It is one of the greatest and wisest expressions — almost a cliché — of investing that *"it is not timing the market that matters, it's time in the market."*

The whole point can be put in a few words (though dozens of useless books have been written on the subject): *timing the market simply does not work.* You may as well predict plane crashes — or plane arrivals and departures during severe snowstorms. Countless research and popular magazine articles over the past several decades have all reached the conclusion that *market timing does not make any sense as an investment strategy.* It is counterproductive; it is wrong hundreds of times for every rare time that it is surprisingly successful. Market timing does not work for **anyone,** even for the so-called Experts in the Field of Investing.

Here are just a few of my favourite statistics:

On the Toronto Stock Exchange, between 1957 and 2004, there was never a period of ten years that had a negative return. If you tried to time the market by jumping in and out of the market over those four decades, you lost your chance to take advantage of those always-positive returns.

One of the most stunning investment studies of all time looked at the very influential Standard & Poor's 500. If you had invested money in that index on the first day of 1993, and sold out on the last day of 1997 — a total of only five years, please note — you would have earned just under 25% each year — inarguably an amazing return.

Over that half decade, the stock market was open for business for a total of 1,262 days. Yet *if you were out of the market for just 10 of those 1,262 days — less than 1% of that period of time — you would have lost 60% of the total profit it made over those five years!* Put another way, that foolish in-and-out, market-timing investor who missed those 10 super days — and who but a gifted fortune-teller can know which days will be great ones on the stock markets of the world? — *still* managed to earn nearly 10% a year (9.8%, to be exact). Now, that certainly beats a GIC or a Canada Savings Bond, but it is *vastly lower* than the 24.6% earned by those who realized that market timing is absurd and useless, and who left their money invested in the index for the whole period, uninterrupted.

If you left your money in over the entire period, and never touched it, you would have seen an average increase of 10.4% a year! The investor who *trusted* the market, riding its often-stomach-churning roller-coaster over all those years, left his or her grandchildren a tidy inheritance. The market timer who panicked with each short-term drop, yanking money out and then throwing it back in, and, of course, paying brokerage fees each time he performed each action, left all those hungry and hopeful descendants not a single penny.

Doesn't Market Timing *Ever* Work?

Has anyone ever made money by timing the market? Of course. There are people who win the lottery, and others who can guess "heads or tails" on a flipped coin nine times out of ten. Of course, flip the coin ten *more* times, and they may guess it right once or twice over that series of tosses, at most. But no one ever talks about that, do they? Indeed, have you ever seen the name of a famous market timer in the *Forbes* "*400 Richest*" list?

Market timing is garbage. It is crystal-ball gazing, and it simply **does not work**. It is, indeed, "time **in** the market" that always, inevitably, pays off, even with all those dips and drops that scare off millions of investors every single year — some of them, sadly but understandably, after the Great Depression, for life.

One of the great mutual fund managers of the past few decades, Peter

Lynch, is also a bestselling author. He may have put it best in one of his impressive books:

> *Since 1965, if you bought stocks once a year and were unlucky enough to pick the worst day to invest (when stocks were at their highest prices) 30 years in a row, you ended up with an annual return of 10.6%. If you were incredibly lucky and invested on the best day of the year, 30 years in a row, you ended up with an annual return of 11.7%. So the difference between perfect timing and horrendous timing is 1.1%. This timing business is much ado about very little.*

Money Solutions Market Timing Highlights
• Market timing does not work. It's that simple.
• As an investment strategy, it fails 99% of the time; its rare success only proves the rule.
• You can never know if the one month — or day — that you choose to sell, and be "out of the market," will be one that experiences record gains.
• Don't allow fears and the inevitable jumps and dips of the world's markets to move you to sell quality stocks. If you *don't* sell, you have lost *only on paper.*

MUTUAL FUNDS

Mutual funds have been hot for Americans and Canadians (and others around the world) over the past few decades. And they don't appear to be cooling; the Investment Funds Institute of Canada reported that *$23.4 BILLION of new money was pumped into mutual funds in this country in 2005 alone,* so the interest in this concept has hardly slowed down. Yet for all the talk, for all the billions that keep pouring in, there is one essential **misunderstanding** about mutual funds: they are *not* an "investment"; they are *a method by which people invest.*

Mutual funds are pools of money, a little bit from each of many thousands of people like yourself, that are allocated to various categories of investments. Possible categories are (in alphabetical order, not necessarily in order of preference):

Bonds
Mortgages
Precious metals
Real estate
Stocks (equities)
Treasury bills.

Any of the above investments, on their own or in combination, can be the underlying investments for a mutual fund. For example, there are mutual funds whose portfolios (or underlying investments) are in bonds; these are therefore called bond funds. There are mortgage funds, whose underlying investments are — you guessed — in mortgages. For those brave hearts who think that owning a diamond ring is the same as investing, there are precious metal funds, with portfolios consisting of gold, silver, etc. And so on.

Taking Stock of a Real Dilemma

Here is an example of the challenges — and confusion — that an investor has to deal with, when trying to decide which actively managed mutual fund to put money into. Just ponder, for a moment, the following list of the funds offered by the top ten mutual fund companies in Canada:

Company	# of Mutual Funds Offered
IGM Financial Inc.	286
RBC Asset Management Inc.	76
C.I. Investments	117
CIBC Asset Management	138
AIM Trimark Investments	54
TD Asset Management Inc.	52
Fidelity Investments Canada Limited	70
BMO Investments Inc.	57
AGF Management Limited	71
Franklin Templeton Investments	72

Which of these hundreds of funds should you choose? And how on earth can you even start to choose? I might note that the largest mutual fund company operating in Canada — IGM Financial — handles over $95-BILLION of its clients' dollars in its 286 (!) different mutual funds. But how different are each of these funds, really?

Now, could you please tell me, *why would anyone want to risk their money in these outrageously complex and confusing investments?* And there is one more very important point to consider: the more funds you have in your portfolio, the greater your risk. This is because *you are nearly always investing in the same stocks through different funds.* For example, if you own more than one Canadian fund, there is a very good chance that you have BCE or Barrick Gold several times in your portfolio. *Is this duplication really necessary, very wise, or very useful?*

The real reason for the awful mishmash of names and fund offerings seems to be that the more mutual fund companies confuse you, the greater will be your dependence on mutual funds salespeople and stock brokers — who, unfortunately, will always be motivated by commissions. Like a new chewing gum flavour, a new kind of diet soda, or new variety of yogurt, a new fund offers new possibilities of sales and profits for their creators.

Profit for Whom?

But will these products offer more possibilities of profits for *you?* The mediocre performance of many funds in the marketplace *also* gets hidden by this continuous introducing of new and "different" funds. How often does a mutual fund "family" publish, and advertise, the performance of **all** of its too-many funds? In those gorgeous, expensive, full-page newspaper ads, you always see only a small number of their best-performing funds shown off, while the others get hidden away, like runts in a litter. Before you put your hard-earned money into any mutual fund, here are some important points to consider:

MERS reduce returns. An M.E.R. (Management Expense Ratio) is basically the fee a mutual fund company charges you to manage your money. Study after study has shown that MERs (which could be as much as 3% or higher annually) *reduce* the return you get on your investment.

You could pay as much as 6% in commissions in year one of your investment. This is *in addition to* the MER. (That's a LOT!)

Past performance of mutual funds is not a predictor of future perform-ance. One of the biggest investment mistakes you can make is to focus on *last year's* mutual fund performance. (Imagine planning for Hurricane Kat-rina in 2005 by basing your preparations on the same month in 2004!) Financial trade publications know that to create a bestselling magazine, all they have to do is place on the cover a lead like *"Ten Hot Funds to Include in Your Portfolio."* But the world's most respected academics have proven, again and again, that *performers in the top 10% in any one year are more likely to fall to the bottom 10% the next, than to reappear in the top 10%!* To put it another way, investing in *last year's* top performers is a crap shoot. Think about it: do you believe, in your heart or even your well-oiled mind, that either the price of gold or the price of oil will increase during 2006 and after, anyway near the way the two rocketed upward in 2005?

Beware of deceptive performance claims. Investment newsletters, mag-azines, glossy mutual fund brochures, full-page ads, and even lengthy books are constantly bombarding investors with promotions of the superior per-formance of some mutual fund. Treat most of what you see as entertainment; certainly, *never* depend on these promotions when you're planning your financial future. Odds are, a great performance was produced over a very short period of time and is *not* sustainable over the long term.

Should you invest in "actively managed" funds or "index" funds? Active managers attempt to uncover securities the market has either under- or over-valued and to *time* their investment decisions in order to be more heavily invested when the market is rising, and less when the market is falling. Examples of actively managed funds are those with high MERs and commissions offered by mutual fund salespeople and stock brokers. Academ-ics in the field of investment have proven again and again that active managers are unlikely to add any value to your investments, because the markets are highly efficient: timing the market, as I've noted above, is a loser's game. The only actively managed funds you should *ever* consider for your investment portfolio are those with the investment philosophy of buy-ing great businesses and holding them for long periods of time. But even these rarely do as well as Index funds.

Index funds are "passively managed" funds that seek to replicate the performance of a particular index (such as the TSE 300; S&P 500; Nasdaq 100; Dow Jones) by buying and holding all the securities in that index, in direct proportion to their weight by market capitalization within the index. Index funds are available from most major banks.

As I will show at much greater depth in **Step 3,** below, **index funds should outperform most actively managed funds,** because *investors, as a group, can do better than the market.* After all, collectively, we *are* the market!

Here's an example of how some of the world's leading indexes have performed recently: The percentage of returns of the MSCI **Europe Index** was 6.09% for 2005, but its three year average was 11.7%, and its *20-year average* was 11.05%; not bad!

The MSCI **Japan Index** was up 21.236% for 2005, and averaged a 13.539% increase over the previous three years.

And *here* is an index that you may recognize: *the S&P/TSX Composite Index Total Return was up 24.129% in 2005, and it averaged 21.662% gain since January of 2002.*

Show these numbers to your risk-averse Canada Savings Bonds holders and T-Bill purchasers, and ask if they should ever be satisfied with low, single-digit returns again.

Money Solutions Mutual Funds Highlights
  • Mutual funds are *not* an investment, but rather a *method* of
  investing.
  • There are *far* too many mutual funds offered, and *far* too much
  confusion about them.
  • Beware of high management expense ratios (MERs), which can
  devastate the annual returns from your funds.
  • Past performance is *never, ever* a guarantee of future success — or a
  reason to choose one mutual fund over another.
  • Becoming informed and knowledgeable will mean that you can
  simplify your investments, recognize the many flaws inherent in most
  mutual funds, and invest more wisely and successfully — preferably
  with ETFs — Exchange Traded Funds — which follow major indices
  of markets (and sectors) in countries around the world, have lower
  MERs and less risk.

OFFSHORE INVESTING

Numerous Canadians, including some of its wealthiest and most prominent citizens, use **offshore investing.** There are many reasons why Canadians — *an*d successful people from other countries around the globe — set up offshore accounts. The Canadian government does not discourage its citizens from investing offshore, but it does not look kindly upon its residents not paying their full complement of Canadian taxes, of course. The basic rule is, all Canadian residents must declare their world-wide income in their annual personal tax return.

Whether you are an individual, a corporation, a trust or a partnership that owns foreign property with a total cost of more than $100,000 any time during the year, you must file a completed form T1135 (a Foreign Income Verification Statement), in which you must report those assets. Foreign bank accounts, shares of foreign corporations, and real estate holdings that are situated outside Canada, will all trigger the reporting rules. Property used exclusively for the purpose of carrying on an active business, funds in registered pension plans, personal use property, and shares in foreign affiliates, are exempt from the reporting rules, however.

Remember that, even if the cost of your foreign assets does *not* exceed $100,000, you must *still* report any income that you earn on these assets. Along with the reporting rules, there are substantial penalties for delayed reporting, under-reporting, and non-reporting of foreign income. Penalties will apply in the case of intentional non-filing for more than 24 months, as well as under-reporting.

Money Solutions Offshore Investing Highlights
>	• Investing offshore is still an attractive option for many Canadians, but you should be aware of the risks involved.
>	• Always try to consult a knowledgeable investment advisor before taking your money outside of Canada.
>	• Your best and easiest method for not having to report is NOT to hold foreign assets that cost more than $100,000.
>	• Because investment in an active foreign business will not trigger the reporting rules, you might consider this as an ideal offshore investment strategy.

OLD AGE SECURITY

Canada has long been proud of its "safety net," even if that financial net has steadily been ripped and shredded over the years.

It was back in 1927 that the federal government first started to supplement provincially administered old-age benefits. **Yet old age security (OAS)** — the modem version dates back to 1952 — has been under attack for several years now, both from without and within: from without, in that Canadians are living longer and healthier than ever before, putting great strain on the system; from within, in that Ottawa briefly considered doing away with OAS in the late 1990s and replacing it with a tax-free Seniors' Benefit system, based on family income — with benefits dropping precipitously for seniors who were well off.

OAS is a **universal benefit,** meaning that it is available to everyone who meets certain residency requirements and is over 65 years of age.

To begin receiving it when you turn 65, however, you must apply for it at least six months before that big birthday, through the federal department of Health and Welfare. Application forms can be found in your neighbourhood post office. You won't get rich from OAS — the maximum monthly payment was under $485 as of the spring of 2006 — but that's not the point. *You are entitled to it.* Why ignore money that you've paid for, over many years, and that you have coming to you? Certain provinces have their own modest supplements; check with your provincial pension office. Your best bet is to call up the website of Social Development Canada (www.sdc.gc.ca) to have most of your questions answered.

OAS is an indexed pension, which means that any increase in the Consumer Price Index will lead to a corresponding adjustment of payments, and this occurs four times a year. Benefits for spouses are also available, depending on age, income and residence, and as the Bible admonishes us, widows are to be provided for, even if they have not worked out of the home.

The Benefit with Sharp Claws
In 1991, the Mulroney government introduced a "clawback" of OAS benefits. Under this law, higher income earners in their senior years have seen their benefits reduced. If your taxable income is over $60,806 (until June, 2006;

the new maximum allowed will be $62,144 from July, 2006 to June 2007), you must pay an additional 15% in taxes on the higher amount — in effect, your benefits are slashed by $15 for every $100 that your income is over this limit. And if your taxable income is above $98,793 (until June 30, 2006; $100,914 until one year later), the entire amount of your OAS will be clawed back.

Ways to Maximize Your OAS Payments

All those years of paying into OAS, and you may lose it all? Is that fair? Maybe not. Either way, tax experts suggest several ways to make your taxable income less, so the claws will dig in a little less deep.

- If you are married, split your income so that the income of the higher earner is lowered. It's also wise to open a spousal RRSP.
- Make sure that you take advantage of every tax deduction and credit that you are allowed — and there are many!
- Make your maximum RRSP contribution in the very first year of your retirement, based on the earnings of your prior year, and maintain your investments in your RRSP as long as you can. If you avoid touching your RRSP for several years, this will (obviously) lower your total income, and either lessen or eliminate the claws of Ottawa's bear on your OAS benefits. Then, at the age of 69, you can convert it into an RRIF (see the entry on these funds later in this section), which enables you to take lower income for the first few years following your retirements.

Help for Low-Income Seniors: The GIS

Whether you are single or married, if you have very little income and receive old age security payments, you are eligible to receive **Guaranteed Income Supplements (GIS).**

A single person may qualify for these monthly payments of $389.23 (on average; the *maximum* monthly benefit is $593.97), if his or her maximum annual income is under $14,256. A married couple may qualify for even higher monthly payments, also on top of OAS. Remember, these supplements are also always increasing by a few dollars, several times a year. But they do not come automatically, so **you must renew your request for GIS**

every year. Here, too, call up www.sdc.gc.ca, or phone 1-800-277-9914, for more information.

One more nice thing: GIS *payments are not taxable;* no claws are out to grab them. Furthermore, several provinces may also have low-income supplements available, so it's wise to check that out, as well. The excellent tax expert Evelyn Jacks has some further advice:

> *Seniors can influence the size of their monthly OAS cheque with proper tax planning. Attempt to stay behind the $53,215 annual clawback threshold by planning to split RRSP/RRIF withdrawals between spouses, diversifying investment income sources, offsetting capital gains with capital losses, and so on. Also be sure to file a tax return every year to receive the benefits on a timely basis. Because clawbacks are determined by what income levels were in the previous year, taxpayers whose income will drop dramatically in the new benefits year may apply to have regular OAS benefits reinstated in hardship cases.*

One of my goals with this book is to assist my fellow Canadians in avoiding the possibility of ever becoming "hardship cases." Still, it's nice to know that all citizens continue to have old age security — and, for those in need, the bonus of GIS — coming to them, if and when they need it.

Money Solutions Old Age Security Highlights
   • Old Age Security (OAS) is "universal" — so far — in that all you
   need is to be 65 years of age and live in Canada for much of the year.
   • OAS won't make you rich, but you *do* have it coming to you. *You paid for it!*
   • There are several simple ways to receive larger OAS payments, such
   as income splitting with your spouse and taking advantage of tax
   deductions.
   • Those with lower incomes can and should take advantage of
   Guaranteed Income Supplements (GIS).

PENSION PLANS

Some financial planners urge smart investors to actually *forget* about their company pension and Canada Pension Plan, suggesting that people see them as merely a "bonus" on top of their "real" potential income flow in their retirement years. This attitude makes a lot of sense. If you *look at your* RRSP after the age of 69 and your RRIF or annuity as your *main source of income* in your later years, you'll probably be a lot more aggressive and active in planning your retirement income.

Company Plans

Less than one in two working Canadians expect to receive a company pension from their employers — 45%, to be more exact. After all, these pension plans are not mandatory. But when they do exist, they can certainly provide a real icing on the cake of one's retirement income. But be aware of the growing number of giant firms (such as major airlines and giant car manufacturers) who have begun to pull back and even shrink their long-standing pension plans. This is not limited to only the United States, so be sensitive to this increasing fact of life.

There are two types of employer-sponsored pension plans, and it helps to know the difference. A **defined contribution plan** does not guarantee any specific benefit at the time of your retirement; it's up to you to choose wise investments. The amount of the pension cheques you will receive in the future will be determined by how much has been contributed in your name, and by the rate of return the plan makes on those contributions over time. Usually, the employer will contribute a percentage of your salary or a flat sum, and you'll be allowed to match it, if you can.

The **defined benefit plan,** on the other hand, has a formula spelled out, and the income you will receive in retirement is guaranteed. This kind of plan is administered by the employer, who makes all the decisions about what to invest and where, and it is he or she who keeps that guarantee. You may *not* be required to make contributions — or you may *have* to. So you'd better find out!

Options for Changing Companies

Most men and women don't stay at the same company for their entire career anymore. As the great Canadian thinker Marshall McLuhan noted wisely, over a generation ago, "People no longer have *careers;* they have *jobs.*" If you leave your job and move on, provided you were there long enough to become eligible for the company's pension plan, there are several possibilities open to you.

You may be able to transfer the pension to your new place of employment, but this rarely works, except in governmental plans. You can transfer your money into a locked-in RRSP, which cannot be touched until you reach the age of retirement listed in your former company's pension plan. You can purchase an annuity with the funds, although here, too, you'll be unable to touch the money until a decade before the retirement age noted in your former company's plan. Or you can leave your pension compounding away in your former employer's plan, and start collecting when you finally retire, later in life.

Payment Options

When you start collecting your pension, you usually have three options as to how you wish to receive those benefits: a pension for life will pay you a set sum every month until your death; a pension for life with provisions for your spouse, children, or estate will also send you a monthly income, but this will continue after your death to your beneficiaries; the joint-and-last survivor option lets both you and your spouse receive payments from the plan as long as either of you remains alive.

The best choice for you will depend on several factors, including your overall financial situation, your health, and your age.

CPP — Three More Initials to Remember!

Whether or not your company has a pension plan, you are eligible for the **Canada Pension Plan** (CPP) (or, for residents of La Belle Province, the Quebec Pension Plan [QPP]). Every Canadian who has worked for either him/herself or for a company is eligible for this; if you were self-employed, you've paid the entire contribution into the plan each month. If you were in the employ of a firm, both of you contributed equally into the Plan.

Although many Canadians continue to retire at 65, the CPP can start flowing as early as age 60 or as late as age 70. Note, however, that *the benefits are reduced if you begin drawing them early* — by one-half of one percent for every month before the age of 65 that you've been drawing your pension, which means a whopping 6% lower sum, annually. Maybe it's worth waiting until the traditional age 65. If you retire *later* than age 65, your pension will *increase* half a percent for every month past that date. The real question is, do you come from a family with good genes and long life spans?

How much you will receive each month naturally depends on how long your working career lasted, and how much you contributed to the plan. The maximum retirement benefit is below $850 a month (for 2006), although the death-benefit lump sum of around $2,500 is always welcome. (A spouse's monthly benefit could reach nearly $475 a month in 2006, and a disability benefit could be over $1,030, based, of course, on one's contributions over the years.)

The CPP has been plagued in recent years by insufficient contributions, poor investment returns, and benefit levels that have often been excessive — especially disability claims. Whether it will survive in its present form, or whether the size of contributions necessary on the part of both employers and employees will have to increase dramatically, are both unknown. What is known is that it is worthwhile to check out the status of your CPP. It's always good to know where your next few hundred bucks will be coming from. Just don't expect it to turn up, gift-wrapped, on your 65th birthday; *you must contact Health and Welfare Canada to start your benefits.* And don't forget that you are also eligible for OAS (see the entry on old age security, earlier in this section and weep). Oh — and **congratulations on your retirement!**

Money Solutions Pension Plans Highlights
• Only 45% of Canadians will receive a company pension when they retire.
• Knowing the difference between defined-contribution plans and defined-benefit plans can be crucial to the fulfilling of your retirement dreams.
• There are many options available for transferring pensions when you change jobs and for eventual payment. Check them out!
• Most Canadians are entitled to receive CPP benefits. But the amount of each cheque is profoundly affected by the age you choose to start drawing it (whether it be at 60 or 70). And you must contact Health and Welfare Canada; they *won't* be calling *you.*

RESPs — REGISTERED EDUCATION SAVINGS PLANS

Big surprise: Education is getting a **lot** more expensive. Thank heaven for RESPs — Registered Education Savings Plans, which are savings programs for post-secondary education which earn tax-sheltered income.

A quick look at the striking increase in the cost of Canadian tuitions over the past few years alone makes one realize that the times are certainly a-changing. It was only a few years ago that the excellent McGill University in Montreal was charging a shockingly low $500 a year in tuition; in 2006, years after the Quebec provincial government started to cut its subsidies to higher education, its annual tuition slowly but surely began to approach the $3,000 range.

On average, tuition for the typical undergraduate program in Canadian universities rose *111%* between 1990 and 2005, and I sense that your income did not rise as much (allowing for inflation). But fees vary a great deal, from coast to coast. True, Quebec students can still pay as little as $2,136 a year at Sherbrooke and $2,842 at Concordia, but other tuitions across our Home and Native Land may shock you: Memorial University in Newfoundland now costs $3,015, Ottawa's Carlton costs $4,691 annually; University of Western Ontario in London is now $5,003, and tuition fees for Dalhousie (Science) and Acadia Universities in Nova Scotia have now reached $7,320 and $8,116, respectively. And that's one year, remember, not the full four years needed to obtain a degree!

The latest projections of Statistics Canada and others suggest that by the time a baby born in 2005 reaches university age, a four-year degree in one of our country's institutions will well exceed $50,000 to $80,000 — over $12,500 to $20,000 a year! And this doesn't count room and board, books, clothes, or other living expenses. *The cost of tuition at Canadian institutions of higher learning is rising at a far higher and faster rate than inflation,* and the results are hitting parental pocketbooks like a ton of very expensive and very heavy bricks.

Of course, maybe your kids won't want a post-secondary education. Maybe they won't get pimples, want to borrow the car, and constantly listen to loud and irritating music, either. But you'd better not count on it. In a national survey conducted by Creative Research International a few years ago, a large number of Canadian youths aged 9 to 14 were asked about their future educational plans. Some findings:

- A full 79% said that they wanted to go to college or university, up from 67% a year earlier. And 98% agreed with the statement "Education is important to my future."
- When asked to respond to the statement "I plan to go to college or university some day," 87% of young people in Atlantic Canada responded in the affirmative, followed by British Columbia's 81%.
- Even in the regions with the lowest rates of positive response — in Ontario and the Prairie Provinces — over 2 out of 3 (77% and 72%, respectively) were still reacting favourably to the idea of seeking out higher education in their future.
- A whopping 91% of young people — over 9 out of 10 — who came from families with incomes of greater than $75,000 a year planned to study beyond high school.
- Even the children of the lowest-income families planned to go to post-secondary institutions, at the rate of 3 out of 4.

The researchers concluded: "The generation between the ages of nine and fourteen are sold on higher education. If you have a teen at home, you might want to start socking away some major money."

What's sad is that it doesn't have to be *major money* that is "socked away," if parents and grandparents — and friends and relatives — start to think of a child's future university education when he or she is born rather than when the kid is already in the "tweens" like the college-hungry young people interviewed in the survey. Options for Registered Education Savings Plans (RESPs) are getting better and more generous than ever before.

Get Out of the Pool
For many, many years, "pooled RESPs," often called "scholarship plans," were exceedingly popular across Canada. You would see their little brochures piled high in your neighbourhood bakery or dry cleaning establishment, and they certainly *looked* very attractive: big photos of a gorgeous baby or toddler, along with words like "the most trusted provider of guaranteed

RESPs." These were savings plans set up as charitable donations, or non-profit companies, and they were a kind of "forced savings" for many hundreds of thousands of Canadian parents who wanted to put away money for their kids' future post-secondary educations.

However, these plans had flaws galore; we urge you, in capital letters: DON'T GO THAT ROUTE! With these pooled plans, or scholarship trusts, you had *no* control over the money, and you *never* knew how much you'd be getting when little Jennifer or Jason finally went off to some kind of college. After all, all the money invested was pooled — hence, the name — so the amount received depended, every year, on how many children participating in that fund were entering university in each particular year.

I know of countless parents who were delighted to "get back" all the money they had invested over the years — the principal — when their child entered his or her first year of post-secondary education, but then were devastated to receive only $600 or so each semester thereafter because of the large number in their pool who were also entering colleges — even as tuitions shot past $3,000 and $4,000 a year.

And then, the most dreadful "catch" of all: If your brilliant but non-academic child decided not to pursue a post-secondary education, you forfeited all the gains made on the years and years of your investments! All that money was redistributed to the *other* plan holders whose children were not "late bloomers" like yours, or were more focused on their educational future. What a waste!

Get out of the pool, and swim in a much healthier pond or lake, like the ones described below.

Extra! Extra! A Government Plan That Actually Helps!

The **Canada Education Savings Grant** (CESG) is designed to help parents save for their child's post-secondary education, and it should not be ignored.

Since 1998, every child residing in this country under the age of 18 that possesses a social insurance number has been eligible for a grant of up to 20% on the first $2,000 made in annual contributions toward his or her RESP. You read that right: Ottawa will add up to $400 a year to the money the child's parents, grandparents, godparents, whoever puts into any RESP, up to a life-time total of $7,200. Who says that governments only take, and never give?

There are, naturally, rules to follow:

• The savings you can put into an RESP is limited to $4,000 per beneficiary, per calendar year, until the child turns 21.
• The plan must be collapsed within 25 years of its start.
• The $400 yearly CESG "gift" from the government is available for every child, but only to the age of 18.
• If withdrawals of capital are made from the RESP before the beneficiary begins a post-secondary education, then the CESG must be repaid. You can easily obtain the complete text of these legitimate and fair rules on the Internet or from your local tax office.

But here is *the greatest advantage of all* — especially recalling those extremely unsatisfactory "pooled" plans or "scholarship trusts" that I warned you against, above: If the beneficiary of these RESPs chooses *not* to attend a post-secondary institution, all the contributions made into that plan — if it has been in effect for at least ten years — can be withdrawn tax-free, then rolled into the contributor's RRSP, or spousal RRSP (the maximum transfer is $50,000), or even cashed in! (Naturally, if all this growth is cashed in, taxes must be paid on it. And if the money is withdrawn for non-educational purposes, the government will hit you with a 20% penalty tax to recoup the CESG).

More good news: This RESP can also be used to cover the education of the parent, grandparent, or generous friend who has been putting in the money. And the definition of "education" can be fairly broad: not only programs in most post-secondary institutions across Canada, but many outside this country are eligible, as long as the programs run several weeks, and are accredited. Exciting examples abound: Adults have been known to use this money for a three-month course on Religious Art in Spain (in Spain), or Modern London Theatre (in London, England!). In other words, even if that gorgeous baby ends up choosing not to go off to university or college, *his or her parents or grandparents* can legally use that RESP to cover tuition, books, room and board, and more, for themselves. Clearly, RESPs are now more flexible than ever before — especially given the kickstart of that annual $400 potential "gift" from the federal government.

Here is a powerful chart to show how easy it could be to send your child to the best university or college with savings of a mere $100 a month:

AN RESP INVESTMENT PLAN ASSUMING 12% RETURN

YEARS	$100/MONTH	$120/MONTH ($100 from you; $20 from government)
1	$1,268	$1,522
2	$2,697	$3,238
3	$4,308	$5,169
4	$6,122	$7,347
5	$8,166	$9,800
6	$10,471	$12,565
7	$13,067	$15,681
8	$15,993	$19,191
9	$19,289	$23,147
10	$23,004	$27,605
11	$27,190	$32,628
12	$31,906	$38,287
13	$37,221	$44,665
14	$43,210	$51,852
15	$49,958	$59,950
16	$57,562	$69,075
17	$66,131	$79,357
18	$75,786	$90,943

Now, it's true: Bill Gates did, indeed, drop out of Harvard. But your kid will probably not be exactly like Bill Gates — and don't forget, the Microsoft Master had parents who had set aside enough money to send the lad to Harvard in the first place.

Education has never been more important. The days of making a living by the literal sweat of one's brow are not entirely over, but pretty close to it. And most of us do *not* want our kids flipping burgers and pouring coffee — honourable professions, true; but most of us, I sense, would prefer if our offspring had opportunities beyond that, given the chance.

Since the Canadian government made those very welcome changes in

1998, RESPs have never made more sense (and the pooled/scholarship ones have never made *less*). A growing number of banks and mutual fund companies offer their own RESP "in trust" accounts, and wise parents should check these out, since RESPs that invest in equities have the greatest chance of growing exponentially over the nearly two decades it takes a baby to grow into a college or university student.

Post-secondary education is going to cost a fortune in the years ahead. To quote one prominent Canadian tax manager, *"RESPs make sense. It is not often that you can earn low tax income and get government grants in the process."* If you plan ahead and avoid the pitfall of "pooled" plans, your child will get the education he/she needs to be able to compete with the other, well-educated young people out there when he/she is eventually out in the marketplace.

Money Solutions RESPs Highlights
- RESPs are now more attractive than ever as tax-sheltered vehicles to save for a child's post-secondary education. It is easy to build very large sums over the nearly two decades from a child's birth to his or her high-school graduation.
- The vast majority of Canadian youth plan to attend *some* kind of college or university, and by the time they turn 18, it will cost tens of thousands of dollars to pay for these programs.
- "Pooled RESPs," also called "scholarship plans," are a disaster. *Don't take that route!*
- The federal government now provides generous grants, called CESGs, to boost your RESP contributions.
- Be aware of the rules and regulations of CESGs.
- Even if your child chooses *not* to continue with his or her education, *other* members of the family who have invested in the RESP will be able to use the money to study, *themselves!*

RRIFs — REGISTERED RETIREMENT INCOME FUNDS

All good things must come to an end. Even an RRSP has a "good until" date stamped on it, like yoghurt; by the end of the year that its owner turns 69, it must be closed, or collapsed. When you reach that point, your long, long days of tax-free contributions into your RRSP will, alas, be legally over. But *not all* of the exciting advantages of your RRSP will have vanished.

You have the option of transferring your money into a **registered retirement income fund**, or RRIF, a tax-deferral vehicle for matured RRSPs. You will no longer be allowed to put any new money into the fund, but your money *will* continue to be grow tax-free, and you *may* continue to invest it in the same kinds of vehicles: stocks, bonds, GICs, mutual funds, and so on. You may also choose to convert your RRIF into an annuity.

So what's the difference between RRSPs and RRIFs, other than the fact that they have slightly different initials, that you are no longer able to contribute more money, and that you are a few years older now? Well, *you are required to withdraw a minimum amount each year from your RRIF* (except the first year that you establish it), and these withdrawals are taxable. The percentage of your fund that you must withdraw is determined by the federal government, and is often changed, so see a good accountant, current tax-planning book, or financial planner for the latest figures.

There are several options available to you once your money is ensconced in an RRIF:

- You may take those payments annually, quarterly, or even monthly.
- You can take them in the forms of various investments that you have made, rather than in cash.
- You'll be able to move your investments out of your RRIF without having to sell them.
- Of course, you'll have to pay taxes on what you withdraw, just as you did on your paycheques in your working days.

Benefits of RRIFs

There are several. Depending on the payment schedule you create and the options you choose, if you've invested wisely, your RRIF may produce a steadily increasing estate for you to live on. Furthermore, *you* completely and totally control the types of investments you wish to have in your RRIF, which you would not be able to do with an annuity.

In a nutshell, you have total control of your RRIF, and may design your own pension — a fact that is very attractive to many older men and women who have the time, energy and interest to watch over and tend the growth of their capital as it continues to compound tax-free.

Are There Drawbacks?

There are certainly *some* disadvantages to RRIFs. For instance, while your RRIF may well provide you with much-needed extra income through your 70s and 80s, they will reach the maximum of 20% of the total remaining, when you turn 94. If you take too much money out each year, you could very possibly outlive your fund. Your RRIF may demand watchful management, depending on the investment vehicles you have chosen and the payment schedule you use. (This is *another* argument for **index funds**; see our discussion of that superior investment vehicle, above, and in **Step 3,** below.)

On balance, however, to quote one financial expert, *"an RRIF, if handled carefully, can be your most valuable source of retirement income."* In many ways, RRIFs are a very attractive continuation of your RRSP, under another name. They can allow you to keep pace with inflation and continue to defer taxes, depending on the amount of your payments. Keep in mind that the size of those regular withdrawals may well reduce your income later in life.

Study the option of purchasing an annuity instead of an RRIF, and make a careful choice. Your final years (and decades!) on this earth, and your comfort during those years, may be dependent upon your decision.

Money Solutions RRIFs Highlights

- RRIFs are a wise tax-deferring vehicle into which you can transfer the funds from an RRSP, which must be collapsed when you reach the age of 69 (annuities are the other main option).
- You will be required to withdraw a minimum amount each year from an RRIF, and that amount *will* be taxed. But new options will be opened to you that you did not have with your RRSP.
- There are both drawbacks and benefits to RRIFs. *Be aware of all of them!*
- An RRIF can be a crucial part of your retirement strategy and contribute to your comfort in your later years.

RRSPs — REGISTERED RETIREMENT SAVINGS PLANS

It is my strong belief that the Registered Retirement Savings Plan (RRSP) should be renamed simply *Registered* Savings Plan (RSP). An RRSP is usually defined as a CCRA/Revenue Canada-approved savings program that allows tax-deferred saving toward one's retirement. But I see it as *so much more.*

It is true that our friendly government, when the RRSP was introduced, wanted us to save for that distant idea of "retirement." But what is retirement? If you had enough money at the age of 40, and wanted to spend the rest of your life doing other things, *would* you retire? Why limit RRSPs to vehicles for our "retirement years" when many of us plan to work — in one way or another — until the day we die?

My point is, there are some common rules that we should all follow when it comes to managing our financial affairs. An RRSP can be used very successfully as an investment and tax-planning strategy, *without any consideration of retirement.* Here's an example for you:

> *Mr. Ted Jones is 30 years of age, and recently married. His wife, Sally Jones, is also 30. Both of them have great jobs, and are in a 35% tax bracket. (See **Step 2, below, on Tax Planning.**)*
>
> *The Joneses are planning to start a family, Sally to stay at home and raise the children until they are of school age. Sally Jones will therefore have no income for several years. Now, here is a marvelous opportunity for smart planning. The Joneses should contribute the maximum possible into their RRSPs when they are both working, even if they have to borrow the money for this-then withdraw the proceeds from Sally's RRSP when she, as a stay-at-home mom, is in a much lower tax bracket. The young couple will then be able to invest those proceeds **outside** her RRSP and reap many benefits,* described later in this section. (Notice how "retirement" in no way comes into this example?)

There are two key components to an RRSP: a tax savings part, and an investment part. Let's look at each one individually.

Tax Savings

Every Canadian who opens an RRSP will get this benefit, and it's a good one. The dollar-amount of the savings depends on your **marginal tax rate** (your tax bracket). If you are earning $50,000 a year and your marginal tax rate is 35%, then for every $1,000 you put into your RRSP, you will save $350 in taxes that year. Not bad!

If you *really* want to maximize the value of your investments, *add* that tax refund (of $350) to the $1,000 you've already put into your RRSP account. You can already see what's happened: Your $1,000 has miraculously turned into $1,350 — *a 35% increase in the value of your RRSP, in just minutes!* That's pretty good financial planning. Now, who needs an advisor, when you now have the knowledge to get this kind of mileage out of your hard-earned income yourself?

Investment

This is the component of the plan in which *the majority of Canadians get short-changed.* Which is a shame, because this aspect is the single most important consideration when it comes to RRSP planning.

Here's an idea that could change the way you manage your RRSP significantly: Treat the funds **in** your plan the same way that you would a portfolio **outside** your plan. Ask yourself the exact same questions, such as "What kind of returns can I expect?"; "What investment risks are involved?"; and "Is the investment strategy I'm considering a proven and successful one?"

According to recent research, most of us don't think about our retirements at all — especially in our youth, but even in our middle years. Hence this terrifying statistic: *82% of Canadian women over the age of 65, and 54% of Canadian men over the same age, rely on government cheques as their only source of cash.* If you've read our section on OAS above, you'll see that this usually amounts to around $500 a month, which doesn't give a senior citizen many trips to restaurants, much less winter flights to Florida, or to visit the grandkids in Vancouver or Halifax.

Here is where an RRSP comes in. *When you register an RRSP with the federal government in Ottawa, you are taking advantage of quite a marvelous tax-saving deal.* You are agreeing to put money away into this plan for use in your retirement years, and not to touch it until then. (Although you *may* choose to do so prematurely for various reasons, such as to make a downpayment on a house, to pay tuition fees, or to make it possible for one spouse to stay at home and raise a family.) Our beloved government will be so touched by your foresight — and so eager to see you saving money that will eventually keep you off the welfare rolls in your later years — that it will offer you a gift as its part of the deal: it will let the money you put into your RRSP grow tax-free, and it will give you a welcome tax deduction each year for your trouble.

Everything You Ever Wanted to Know About RRSPs. . . .

1. An RRSP is *not* an investment. It's a strategy that allows you to save taxes and defer the gains *on* your investment until you withdraw the funds. When does it make sense to withdraw your funds? When your marginal tax rate is *lower* than it was when you made your contributions.

2. Don't just look at RRSPs as funding your eventual retirement. Use them as a tax planning vehicle as well.

3. Make sure you maximize the return on your RRSP funds. Qualifying investments include, but are not limited to, bank savings accounts, GICs, T-bills, bonds, mortgages, and stocks. You can, of course, choose a low-fee mutual fund that invests in one or any combination of these. Or you can keep things simple (and wiser) and use an indexing strategy. Or my beloved ETFs.

4. Make contributions early in your career, and contribute as much as possible every year. Compound growth can work wonders in your portfolio when you do this.

5. Consider making your contributions early in the year; don't wait until the deadline of February 28 of the following year, as most Canadians do.

6. Your contribution limit is 18% of your earned income. There are some other factors that could affect how much you can contribute; your current tax assessment will indicate your current allowable contribution amount.

7. Generally, if you contribute *less* than your RRSP deduction limit, you can carry forward the excess indefinitely (until the age of 69).

8. If you are married and your spouse's income is lower than yours, consider making a spousal contribution.

10. If you don't have the funds available, you should consider borrowing to make your contribution. Use your tax refund to start repaying the loan. And remember, the interest cost is *not* tax deductible.

An RRSP is a powerful tax and investment planning tool. Use it to your advantage, before the government takes that money away in the form of taxes. Don't make your bank, your insurance agent, or your mutual fund salesperson rich; make *yourself* rich!

Money Solutions RRSPs Highlights
- RRSPs are not an investment, but a great strategy to save on tax and defer your gains.
- RRSPs allow tax-deferred saving, but you need not wait until retirement to take advantage of them!
- These vehicles can be an important part of a successful investment and tax-saving strategy.
- Smart people put the taxes they save by investing in an RRSP right back into the plan.
- Ask the same thoughtful questions about your investments, both inside or outside an RRSP.
- Try to maximize your return; invest as early as possible each year (in March or April), and put in as much money as you can, up to the government limit.

THE RULE OF 72

The founder of the great Doyle Dane Bernbach advertising agency, William Bernbach, once protested that "Rules are prisons." And maybe he was right: there are many times in our lives when rules can be confining and crippling. After all, if we all followed to the letter *every one* of the "rules" set down by our parents and teachers, society would never change or improve. But now and then, the world *does* provide us with a wonderful, helpful rule — and, in the case of the Rule of 72, a powerful, potentially life-saving one.

All numbers have *some* kind of mystical value or quality to them: think of the 6 days of creation, the 40 days of rain and the 10 commandments of the Hebrew Testament, or the 40 days Christ wandered in the desert and the 12 Apostles in the Christian one. *The number 72 has an amazing ability to help all of us rule our financial futures rather than have the future rule us.* This rule is *never* broken, because it is a result of mathematical logic. And who would want to break it, since it can assist us so beautifully in planning for the future?

The **Rule of 72** is, simply, that *the length of time it takes for any investment to double in value is equal to 72 divided by the annualized rate of return of your investment.* So, for example, if you have an investment that gives you 8% annually, then, using this magical rule, you promptly know that it will take nine years for it to double in value (72 divided by 8 equals 9).

The Rule of 72 will not guarantee you wealth, but it certainly underlines the tremendous impact of compound interest (which is so important, I give it a Step of its own: **Step 5**). As Allen B. Clarke, a fine Canadian money manager and author, puts it, the Rule of 72 is "a quick mental tool to check how well you have done or where you should be in a certain number of years."

For many investors, this rule, far from being a prison, has the possibility of freeing us all from poverty in our retirement years.

Money Solutions Rule of 72 Highlights
• The Rule of 72 is a simple way to keep track of the success of your investments.
• This magical rule underlines the powerful impact of compound growth.
• Divide 72 by the annualized rate of return of your investment to get the number of years necessary for it to double.

SEGREGATED FUNDS

Segregated Funds are **mutual funds with a life-insurance policy wrapped around them,** which makes them an ideal investment strategy for conservative investors who want to protect their investment from "downside" risk. Segregated Funds offer guarantees and safeguards that regular mutual funds do not match. Here are some of the *major benefits* of this impressive investment strategy:

- **Maturity Guarantee** — Most funds give you the option to guarantee 75% or 100% of your principal (less withdrawals and fees) at maturity, 10 years from the date of contract issue.
- **Death Guarantee** — If the owner of the fund dies within the ten-year period, the beneficiary of the investment will receive either the current market value or the original investment, whichever is greater.
- **Creditor Protection** — If you declare bankruptcy, your Segregated Fund will be shielded from your creditor's reach, as long as the fund was purchased a year earlier and you have a named beneficiary.
- **Probate Fees Exemption** — By naming a beneficiary to receive the death benefit under the policy, an investor may be able to bypass probate fees.
- **Insurance Protection** — To the extent that the Maturity and Death Benefit Guarantees of Segregated Funds are applicable, these same amounts are covered up to $60,000 by Comp Corp, the Insurance Company Protection Association.
- **Tax Benefits** — Income made by a Segregated Fund is allocated monthly, so you don't have to pay tax on gains that arose before you owned units, as you would have to do with mutual funds. Also, if a Segregated Fund loses capital in a given year, the unit holders can claim capital gains made on other investments. Taxation rules allow the allocation of capital gains or losses without cashing in units held. **Mutual Funds do NOT have this ability.**
- **Lower Fees** — Management fees on most Segregated Funds are lower than many mutual funds.
- **Wide Range of Investment Options** — Investors have a wide range of investment options with Segregated Funds when using

the preferred strategy of "passive" investing, versus "active" investing. You know which one *I* love! Here are several seg-funds which I can recommend wholeheartedly — all of them offered by the Industrial Alliance Insurance Company:
• In Bonds: **Bond Fund (series 2)**
• In Canadian Income Trusts: **Diversified Income**
• In Canadian Equities: **Canadian Equity Index**
• In Canadian Real Estate: **Real Estate Income**
• In International Equities: **International Equity Index;**
  U.S. Equity Index; and U.S. DAQ Index.

Money Solutions Segregated Funds Highlights
  • **Seg Funds are far superior investments to Mutual funds.**
  • **Seg Funds offer benefits that cannot be matched by Mutual funds.**
  • **Choose index-based seg funds over actively-managed ones.**

SYSTEMATIC WITHDRAWAL PLANS

This is another of those financial terms which can be life-changing as well as enhancing, and deserves an entire section of its own. See Step 7, below.

WRAPS

The mutual fund industry is always looking for new ways to expand the lists of "products" they offer the public, and one of the hottest in recent years is the so-called **wrap account** (also called a **managed fund,** since actual money managers, not just financial planners, direct these accounts for their clients). Wrap accounts first appeared in the mid-1970s; today, well over $200 billion is handled this way in the United States, and a rapidly increasing amount in Canada.

With a wrap account, an investor receives various investment services, and even brokerage services, all of which are personalized to a certain extent, for a single price — i.e., "wrapped together." This predetermined price can vary greatly, much like the cost of a house mortgage, so *it's essential to shop around in the wrap world.* It's usually a percentage of the invested assets, traditionally ranging up to 3% annually.

Advantages of Wraps

Some would say that wraps are like a map — nice to have, but only if you are totally lost. So, *if you lack the time and inclination to do lots of research on your own about how to invest, maybe a wrap account is worth it to you.*

The "traditional" wrap account was mainly for big players — anything less than $100,000 was not accepted; $200,000 was the usual minimum investment. What an investor got for this expensive advice seemed impressive: serious and frequent consulting, money management, transaction costs, performance monitoring four times a year, and more. A money manager allocated the assets to reach the client's goals in ways that matched his or her needs and tolerance of risk.

It sounded good, so it didn't take long for another kind of wrap to become popular, one that would accept investments as little as $20,000 or even $10,000: **a mutual fund wrap account,** which included most of the services that the big spenders got, but also asset allocation, a customized portfolio of stocks, and more. Many clients liked the idea of having their funds managed with the skill and expertise of a professional money-management firm.

Disadvantages of Wraps

The high cost of these "services" has always been a major rap against wraps. Yet the fees can be negotiable; in recent years, major firms have announced *quite low* wrap fees-not much more than 2% — for "moderate growth portfolios," and even less for "a fixed income pool." Shop around!

But far too many of these wraps hit their clients with extra fees for services — and that deadly MER (management expense ratio) is still paid to fund managers *before* the wrap fee is deducted.

There are other negatives as well. Wrap fees are not always tax deductible. The tax reporting requirements can be huge, since the money manager is often buying and selling stocks on your behalf, and you may be flooded with paperwork from all the trades executed. Wrap contracts can be tough to break and expensive to cancel, if you change your mind. And it's hard to track the performance of your wrap account, since you get those statements only quarterly. Furthermore, moving from stocks or mutual funds into a wrap program can be costly, since you may need to sell off your investments in order to transfer into one, triggering large capital gains and increased taxes.

Proceed with Caution

If you still want to get involved with a wrap, here's how — but *just be careful*. Wrap funds are sold by brokerage houses, mutual fund companies, banks, and private money managers, so you won't have any trouble finding them. They are hardly a scam; they have satisfied the investing needs of a growing number of Americans and Canadians for decades. But there's a lot of hype about them too, and it's important to check out any wrap account you are considering carefully, and read the seller's prospectus — even more closely than you read the ones put out by mutual fund companies.

If being risk averse is the most devastating reason why investors lose money in the market, wrap accounts can impose a much-needed discipline on their owners. After all, millions regularly suffer panic over suddenly dipping stock prices, which leads them to dumping their shares prematurely, and then instills them with a fear of returning to the market. This fear of risk nearly always leads to sacrificing a potential fortune when the market turns around — and it *always* does. But is this discipline worth thousands of dollars a year? Two to three percent on a $100,000 or $200,000 minimum investment ain't cheap.

All the financial experts I have spoken with agree on two things: the benefits of wrap accounts — beyond peace of mind and time saved — are limited. People who are willing to take the time to learn the fundamentals can do their own investing quite nicely, thus saving the $10 to $30 per thousand that wraps all charge. That's just too much money for too few advantages.

Money Solutions Wraps Highlights
- **Wraps — or managed funds — are more popular than they are worthwhile.**
- **Wrap accounts provide several Investment services all "wrapped" together in an often-costly package.**

• Traditional wraps were once only for the upper-middle-class and wealthy investor. Now, they are available for the common folk as well.
• There are certainly some advantages to wraps, but the disadvantages far outweigh those.
• Wraps *can* provide discipline for some skittish investors — but at what cost?

STEP 1

PROTECT YOUR FAMILY'S FUTURE WITH LOW-COST LIFE, DISABILITY AND CRITICAL CARE ILLNESS INSURANCE

A: WHY INSURE?

What can't be cured, must be insured.

— OLIVER HERFORD (1863-1935), U.S. AUTHOR

Forget what you know, or what you *think* you know, about insurance. Ignore what you've heard from insurance agents. Put aside your biases. In this major Step — and it's not by chance that it is *Step 1* — I am going to tell you **the truth** about insurance — including things that your insurance agency would rather you didn't know.

If, after reading what I have to say about mutual funds, you now think that they put investors in a no-win situation, just wait until you read the truth about insurance — especially life insurance! The way that kind of insurance is sold is leaving far too many people either under-insured or owning the wrong type of insurance for their needs. No matter what you've been told, **there is one reason, and one reason only, for buying insurance: to protect against a financial loss.** If there is no potential for financial loss, you simply do not need any insurance. Financial losses can occur if you die, are injured, or become sick. They can also be incurred if your property is damaged, destroyed, or stolen, or if you get sued. You must protect yourself financially in case any of these events occur. The best way to do this is by purchasing insurance to protect the amount, or value, of the asset that is at risk.

The Basics

Before getting caught in the morass of the insurance industry, ask yourself three basic questions:

1. *Why* do I need insurance?
2. *How much* insurance do I need?
3. *What type* of insurance should I buy?

Once you have answered these questions (don't worry if you aren't sure about the answers right now, especially #2 and #3; the rest of Step 1 will help you gain the knowledge you need to determine these answers), you'll know what you are looking for. Then make sure that you shop around for the best possible deal; the Internet makes it fairly easy these days to compare quotes from several companies. All insurance is *not* created equal.

Always work with an independent insurance agent or broker. These men and women represent many carriers, so they are free to shop the market for the best policy for you and your needs. *Never use an agent who represents only one company!*

Now, let me help you make your way through the often confusing world of insurance. You will read about life insurance, why you need disability insurance and what factors you should consider, and a relatively new, but useful offering: critical care insurance.

Money Solutions Why Insure? Highlights

- **The only reason to buy insurance is to protect against financial loss. No other reason is worthwhile considering.**
- **All insurance is NOT created equally.**
- **Never use insurance agents who represent only one company.**
- **Never rely on the Internet to purchase an item of such importance to your life. Would you buy a house or car with only a few clicks, and no way to verify their quality? Always — *always* — seek the advice of a trusted advisor — *in person*.**

B: LIFE INSURANCE

Life insurance plays a very important role in your financial life. While many people seem to find it confusing, the concepts involved are really not difficult. The hard part is wending your way through the maze of different deals available, and making sure you get what you need, no more and no less, for the best price possible. But *the "best price" may not always be the lowest one!* Price is important, but contractual provisions can be *more* important. A simple example: In a joint last-to-die contract, the accumulated cash value should be paid out to the surviving spouse **tax-free.** Yet this crucial fact is not clearly definied in *some* Universal Life contracts! Other contracts may offer the cash pay-out tax-free in the event of **either** insured's disability, but will you know this for sure? You'd better! *Be aware of all contractual provisions!*

How Are Insurance Rates Determined?
This is one very important issue that you should understand before we proceed.

Most insurance companies use three factors to determine how much you pay for life insurance:

1. mortality rates — the number of people who will probably die at each specific age (this is what actuaries figure out);
2. investment returns — the profit that the insurance companies receive by investing your premium over the years; and
3. operating expenses — the cost of running their business.

Although factors 1 and 2 have been working in favour of the public during recent years (people have been living longer, and the stock markets did remarkably well through most of the 1990s), these benefits have not been passed on to the public to the extent that they should be. I will show you why this is true, below.

Types of Life Insurance
There are two basic different categories of life insurance: term insurance and permanent insurance. Both have their advantages, but the former is often all that the average or low-income person may need. Let's take a look at both kinds.

Term insurance (sometimes called **temporary insurance**) covers you for a specified period of time. It is inarguably the lowest-priced, but it has a serious disadvantage: *It can run out before you do!* I was shocked to discover statistics recently that showed *only about 3 people in every 1,000 who purchase term insurance ever get paid!* Because of advancing age (and always increasing cost), most owners of term insurance eventually cancel their policy; others cannot afford to renew it, and many, as I noted sadly, outlive it. Term insurance comes in three flavours:

> **annual renewable term,** the cost of which can go up each year as you grow older (although this is not always the case, because of the savings to insurance companies discussed above);
> **level term,** which locks in the cost for a specific period of time, such as 5, 10, 15, or 20 years, or until you reach a specified age, such as *65 or 80;* and
> **decreasing term,** which is probably the least attractive of all, since your coverage is reduced over time while the premium remains fixed.

Permanent life insurance, in past years, has often *not* been in the best interest of most people, but "products" have gotten much better recently. Here, too, there are three types:

> • **whole life,** which insures you, as the name implies, for your entire life;
> • **universal life,** which was invented by the insurance industry to improve the quality of offerings in "permanent life insurance," *and it has;* and
> • **variable life,** which allows you to invest your "excess" premium in mutual funds.

Whole life insurance is usually defined as life insurance that remains in force during the insured's entire lifetime, while building a savings element (the "cash value").

Universal life policies contract for a certain amount of life insurance coverage, but also include additional premiums to "invest" in a portfolio within that policy. In other words, universal life has *two* components: a term-insurance one and an investment one. I cannot deny it: I used to frown on *all* permanent life insurance, but I've come to recognize just how much better the insurance products have become. Individuals now have considerable choice as to where they can invest the cash component of their insurance policy, and there is a real bonus: **any accumulated growth inside your universal life policy is tax-deferred,** and your returns, if paid to your beneficiary at death, are tax-free. (No, the premiums are *not* tax-deductible.) Within 10 or 15 years, once may withdraw money without penalty, so these are long-term investments, but it can be a superior way of saving (and growing) large sums of money OUTSIDE your RRSP. A dear friend, Anwar Rabah, of Magnum Wealth, a most trustworthy man with over two decades of expertise in this industry, told me recently, *"In a $100,000 policy, the growth in a universal life policy over 30 years could be 100% greater than in a non-registered equity mutual fund."* What I've grown to admire in universal life policies is their new flexibility, and the way they can — essentially for middle- and upper-income people — not only provide insurance protection which both spouses and dependents need, but have tax advantages that can far, far surpass conventional investments.

The Truth About Life Insurance

When I wrote about this major industry several years ago, I was savagely critical. After all, when I worked briefly as an insurance salesman myself, as a young man, I was urged by my bosses to sell only permanent insurance (no, Universal Insurance did **not** exist back then), because — understandably — it paid much higher commissions. And there are still some things that I argue against and for, in this field:

> • Don't believe the nonsense that term insurance should be avoided entirely, because it is only "temporary insurance." Isn't insurance on your car temporary until you renew it each year? And how about the insurance you pay annually on your house? For younger men and women — especially those who have little disposable income to play with — there is no reason why they should not buy term insurance for a specific purpose, and for a specific period of time. *Don't pay for something you may*

never need! I urge those people to consider renewable term insurance, to cover all their life insurance needs. When they have more money to spend and invest, universal life policies could prove to be invaluable-in every meaning of that word.

• Insurance on the life of your child may *seem* like a rip-off, since no one wishes to think of "making money" on the loss of a loved one. But hundreds of thousands of wise parents choose to purchase some kind of permanent insurance for their children when they are very young. This way, *the rates are strikingly low, and the compounding effect on every investment dollar in the contract can grow substantially over the long term.* This action also protects the child's insurability if (heaven forbid) the hazards of disease or serious illness may arise in their young lives. And it provides the child with *further* insurance, and at a lower cost, as Jason or Jennifer ages.

• Shop around for life insurance the same way that you shop around for car or house insurance. There is very little difference, and do not let your agent convince you otherwise. In fact, ask your agent to *show you the quotes* that he or she has obtained on your behalf.

• When in doubt, get a second or third, even a fourth opinion. You will be glad you did, and this little bit of research and questioning could well save you a fortune.

Because the insurance industry has traditionally done such a weak job of educating the public, far too many Canadians either lack adequate life insurance coverage, or are not insured at all. This is too bad, and potentially tragic, because, for an amazingly small monthly premium, you can protect your spouse and children in the event of your untimely death. *Don't* leave your loved ones in need, and *don't* pay more than you should for protecting them!

I cannot overemphasize the importance of shopping around for the best quotes, and of asking the right questions. Make sure you understand what kind of insurance you're getting, and that it's what you need — and don't pay more than you should for protecting your loved ones!

How Much *Do* You Need?

Here is a simple form to help you determine how much life insurance you might need. Just fill in the blanks, then add them up to get the total.

Funeral Expenses, etc.: _____

Final Expenses: _____

Mortgage: _____

Other Debts: _____

Emergency Fund: _____

Education Fund: _____

Adjustment Period: _____

Charitable Gifts: _____

TOTAL CASH REQUIRED: _____

Add to the above one more crucial question: *how much insurance will the surviving family need, to be able to continue to live in the way in which they are accustomed?* After all, their lives will go on, and they will need a regular supply of cash over the years, even decades, ahead. **Speak to a knowledgeable advisor!**

What Will It Cost?

To give you an idea of what term insurance costs, I have put together a chart for your reference, thanks to my friend Anwar. The following assumes that you are a male, in good health, and a non-smoker, of course. If so, and if you are paying much more than the rates listed below, shop around!

ANNUAL PREMIUM FOR 10–YEAR RENEWABLE TERM

AGE	AMOUNT	PRICE	AMOUNT	PRICE	AMOUNT	PRICE
30	$300,000	$221	$500,000	$260	$1-million	$510
35	$300,000	$230	$500,000	$290	$1-million	$570
40	$300,000	$293	$500,000	$385	$1-million	$750
45	$300,000	$413	$500,000	$565	$1-million	$1100
50	$300,000	$596	$500,000	$865	$1-million	$1710
55	$300,000	$875	$500,000	$1355	$1-million	$2690
60	$300,000	$1394	$500,000	$2230	$1-million	$4420
65	$300,000	$2294	$500,000	$3730	$1-million	$7420

Getting Quotes and Purchasing the Policy

Once you have determined how much life insurance you need, you can obtain quotes from the Internet. Then contact an insurance agent and make sure that he or she sells you the insurance you *need*.

Money Solutions Life Insurance Highlights

- You should understand the difference between term insurance and permanent insurance; both have their advantages and disadvantages.
- Never think of the concept of purchasing permanent insurance on your young children's lives as being morbid or calculating. It could well save them large sums of money when they themselves wish to buy insurance in the decades ahead — and the money invested from those early years can grow expotentially over their lives!
- A ten-year renewable term policy is all that most younger people need, or even can afford. Young married couples in their 30s can be covered for hundreds of thousands of dollars, to protect their spouse, and their children, for as little as a dollar a day or less. That is a *lot* of protection for your loved ones for a very tiny amount. *As they grow older, and have more disposable income, they can always look at the fabulous investment potential in Universal Life policies.*

C: DISABILITY INSURANCE

We often joke about being scared of catching a cold or the flu, and laugh at the old uncle who is always complaining about his aches and pains and the dozens of pills he takes every day. But becoming so ill that we are disabled is certainly no laughing matter. As I was finishing up this book in early 2006, a new Statistics Canada report was released, proclaiming the following: *"Poor health drove almost one in five people between the ages of 50 and 69 out of the workforce by 2003. Chronic conditions such as arthritis, rheumatism, high blood pressure and back problems were among the common ailments cited by the almost 470,000 individuals in the 50-to-69 age group who were not working for health-related reasons.*" Nearly one-in-five workers forced off the job! That is hardly a chance or occasional occurrence, is it?

You may be surprised to learn that your largest financial asset is *not* your house, your cottage, your car, even your company pension. Rather, if you are working, *your largest asset is almost certainly your ability to produce an income.* Thus, **the most important type of insurance you can get is disability income insurance!**

Everyone Needs It

You need disability insurance **far more** than another kind of insurance — more than life, health, homeowners', or even auto insurance. Yet *close to one-half of working Canadians do not carry disability insurance, either privately or through work!* There are two main reasons why not; let's look at them both.

Reason #1: It Won't Happen to Me!

Oh? Read these statistics, and if you don't weep, then at least shudder a bit: *48% of all mortgage foreclosures on houses in Canada are caused by disability.* With no income, a family cannot make their mortgage payments. Furthermore, according to recent research, *about 90% of families in which a disability occurs suffer from a marriage breakup.* (So much for the "in sickness and in health" line in many wedding ceremonies!) There are actuaries who make their living from figuring out things such as how long smokers will live on average, what percentage of sisters of victims of breast cancer may be struck by the disease themselves, how long someone in their mid-60s with poor health is likely to live, and so on. The results of their research into the chances of disability are quite shocking, but these recent statistics tell the real story:

- A 35-year-old has a 50% chance of a disability lasting 90 days or longer;
- 1 in 4 Canadians will contract heart disease;
- Of those who are diagnosed with heart disease, 1 in 2 are under the age of 65;
- If you do become totally disabled before you turn 65, the chances of the disability lasting 90 days or longer are nearly

60% for 25-year-olds, 50% for 35-year-olds, 33% for 50-year-olds, and nearly 25% for 55-year-olds; and
• If your disability does last longer than 90 days, the average length of your being out of the work force is 2.1 years if you're 25, 3.1 years if you're 40 or 50, 2.6 years if you're 55, and 1.6 years if you are 60.

Imagine the ramifications of being disabled, and without earnings, for one, two, or three years, even more! No matter **how** successful your career has been to that terrifying moment, your living expenses and other financial obligations could soon exhaust your savings and jeopardize all that you've worked so very hard to create.

Here is where it gets really interesting, and even mind-boggling. Another study shows that *the chances of someone becoming disabled for at least three months before the age of 65 are one in eight.* Yet, the chance of someone's house burning down is less than one in a thousand. But guess how many people have fire insurance on their homes? Close to 100%. And how many have disability coverage? *Barely over one-in-two!*

Reason #2: It's Way Too Costly
It is true that disability insurance does not come cheap, especially compared with term life insurance. The reality is, one really cannot afford to live *without* it.

Group Disability Insurance
Many people who do have disability insurance acquired it because it is provided by their employer. These group insurance plans have a few problems that you should be aware of:

• The cost of the coverage can increase.
• Your employer has the right to cancel it at any time.
• The insurance company can cancel the benefit at any time.
• If you leave that employer, you lose your benefit. (Of course, you do *not* lose the chance that every human being has — of becoming disabled during your lifetime.)

74

Factors Affecting Disability Insurance

You may need some help from a trusted insurance advisor to help you find the best possible disability coverage. Remember to shop around. I cannot stress enough, however, that with disability insurance, unlike with life insurance, cost should *not* be your only consideration. There are several other questions that you should take into account:

1. **How does the policy define "disability"?** The concept of *life* insurance is simple: you die, they pay. Disability insurance is a little less cut and dried; there are all kinds of interpretation of what constitutes disability. For example, if you are an accountant and you lose a finger, are you disabled? Maybe you can find a job as a math teacher. It is important to check things like this carefully, before purchasing a policy.

2. **What is your occupation?** The more dangerous your job, the more likely you'll be hurt, and thus, the more expensive the disability policy. Professional mountain climbers and bomb disposal experts, beware!

3. **Does the policy include inflation protection?** As I discussed in the entry for inflation in the first section of this book, inflation is *the* silent financial killer of the world economy. Check to make sure that your payments are indexed against inflation. This means that they should increase as the cost of living index increases.

4. **What is the waiting period?** You can set the length of time it takes for your benefit payments to start: 30 days, 60, 90, etc. Naturally, the shorter the period, the more expensive the premium.

5. **Does your protection increase as your income grows?** Look for a disability policy that will let you increase your coverage to keep pace with your (hopefully) increasing income.

6. **What is the length of the period for which benefits are paid?** Try to ensure you get a policy that pays benefits to the age of 65.

7. **Will the policy pay a partial benefit if you are partially disabled?** If you are injured and your doctor wants you to work no more than a few hours a day or week — as opposed to your reg-

ular work week — you may not receive any benefits from your coverage. Again, check this out carefully before you buy a policy.

8. Is your policy both guaranteed and non-cancellable? Guaranteed means that the cost of the policy cannot rise. **Non-cancellable** means that you are covered for as long as you can pay your premium.

I have been impressed with Manulife Financial's Disability Insurance, and I appreciate their "Disability Needs Analysis Calculator" — to help you figure out the amount of income you would need, if a disability prevents you from working — available on the Manulife.com website. But that's one of the joys of the Internet; you can check out many different plans — just make sure that you do check Disability Insurance out!

Money Solutions Disability Insurance Highlights

• **The largest asset in your life is not your home or car, but rather your ability to provide an income.**

• **A 20-year-old man is three times more likely to be disabled for at least three months than to die before the age of 65, while a 35-year-old woman is seven times more likely to suffer a long-term disability than to die by that age! The chances of someone being disabled before the age of 65 are a shocking one in eight. Over one-third of any group of men and women between the ages of 45 and 65 will become diabetic and/or and contract heart disease. Yet only one in seven Canadians purchases disability insurance.**

• **Shop around to get the best coverage for the best price in this crucial area of insurance. You may need the help of a trusted insurance professional.**

• **There are several things you should consider when purchasing disability insurance in addition to cost, including the definition of "disability," your occupation, inflation protection, increased protection with income growth, the length of the benefits, and a guaranteed and non-cancelable policy.**

D: CRITICAL CARE INSURANCE

We *are* living longer, at least in many First World nations, like Canada. This is wonderful news. But it also means that the chances of our falling victim to various kinds of critical illnesses has increased exponentially. (Most women suffered *no* problems with menopause only a century or two ago. Why? Because the majority of them died before ever reaching that stage of life.)

So it's marvelous to hear that there has been a veritable explosion of "critical illness insurance products" onto the Canadian market during the past half-dozen years.

Note that I am *not* talking about disability insurance; for that discussion, see above. Disability insurance replaces your income if you become disabled in some fashion and are unable to earn the living you once did.

Critical care insurance provides you with extra funds should you fall victim to a serious disease. A basic plan usually covers cancer, heart attacks, and strokes. There are options for covering other life-threatening illnesses, for which lump-sum payments can be available. Naturally, as with most insurance vehicles, further options can be purchased, such as the return of the premium (under certain circumstances), waivers, and more.

Where Can I Go For Critical Care Insurance?
The answer naturally depends on what plan you are considering. Ones which are most often suggested by people in the insurance industry whom I respect the most, include Industrial Alliance's "Transition Critical Illness Insurance," which provides one with a lump-sum payment after a critical illness is diagnosed. To quote their material, "as a result, you can devote 100% of your energies to your recovery, without worrying about the financial impacts of the illness." (Call up www.inalco.com for more information.)

Royal Bank also is well-respected in this field, and www.rbcinsurance.com will allow you to check out the RBC Insurance comprehensive Critical Illness Recovery Plan policy. (And when you encounter "approximate costs" such as $80,000 a year for daily nursing care, up to $10,000 for a wheelchair, and $30,000 to $100,000 for home modifications for wheelchair accessibility, you realize just how devastating a serious illness can be-to you and your family.)

Worth Your Consideration

Insurance companies are out to make money, which is fine. This is a capitalistic society that we live in. These new kinds of critical care insurance — and there will probably be dozens offered in the next few years — do not come cheap. But neither does catastrophic illness, which can destroy a family's livelihood and savings in a very short period of time. As one insurance expert has noted, these new policies are for "individuals whose other coverage plans do not provide lump-sum payments to cover expenses such as treatment outside Canada, home modifications, domestic help, and business expenses caused by the policyholder's impairment."

In other words, these new critical-illness insurance policies can meet the needs of people who have no access to disability insurance, such as homemakers, who do not qualify for disability insurance because they have no income, but for whom a serious illness would nonetheless carry catastrophic expenses.

Our population is aging. Prescription drugs are skyrocketing in cost, and new, even more costly ones are coming out almost daily. Furthermore, a growing number of Canadians have good cause to worry about cutbacks in provincial health-care plans. Our health system is badly in need of an overhaul; we all know this. I don't mean to sound like a pushy insurance salesman trying to sell you a policy. I am just trying to confront the very real possibility that you, your spouse, or an immediate member of your family may be struck with some kind of critical illness during your lifetimes. And thanks to a growing number of smart insurance companies and banks, insurance coverage for this eventuality is now, finally, being offered.

George Burns was known to joke, "If you live to the age of a hundred you have it made, because very few people die past the age of a hundred." Cute. And Burns himself very nearly made it to 100 (and he smoked cigars since his childhood; no one ever said that life was fair). Alas, the strong genes and good health granted to George Burns are rare; few of us will probably spend our last days as he did, working on stage and in movies until only a few days before dropping dead at age 99. With this fact in mind, critical care insurance is certainly worth your careful consideration.

A Final Word On Planning

I hope STEP 1 has made clear to you why insurance planning is one of the most important "money solutions" decisions you can make in your life. Why work all those years to see your savings vanish in a split second? I am convinced that a lot of insurance is bunk — unnecessary and overpriced; a pure waste of money. But *some of it is essential.* I recommend term life insurance, and universal life — *if* you can afford to invest that way; disability insurance, and critical care insurance to protect yourself and your loved ones against serious financial loss in the case of real catastrophe. Give the possibilities lots of thought and some action. And **get cracking on studying the various offerings, comparison shopping, and purchasing some sensible plans.**

This is one situation where I would never want to say to anyone — or even think to say — I told you so.

Money Solutions Critical Care Insurance Highlights

• More and more Canadian companies — both insurance firms and banks — are offering critical care insurance; I strongly recommend you give this type of insurance careful consideration.

• Critical illness insurance plans usually cover cancer, heart attacks, and strokes by default. But it usually pays out the insured amount on diagnosis of nearly two dozen serious illnesses, often within 30 days of diagnosis.

• These new products are specifically designed to meet the needs of individuals and homemakers who have no access to any kind of disability insurance, which you must have an income to qualify for.

STEP 2

REDUCE YOUR TAXES AND CREATE MORE MONEY FOR INVESTMENTS, AND A BETTER LIFESTYLE

A: PAYING OUR DUES

Noah must have taken into the ark two taxes — one male and one female.
And did they multiply bountifully!

— WILL ROGERS, AMERICAN HUMORIST, 1879-1935

Taxes, taxes and more taxes. It seems as if they're everywhere, and there is nothing we can do to escape them. There's income tax — federal, provincial, and sometimes even municipal. Then there's the GST, not to mention gas taxes, surtaxes, alternative minimum tax, capital gains tax, tax on dividends, tax on interest. And on and on. And on.

It seems as though every single time our governments need more money — usually due to mismanagement — they find new ways to tax us and new things to tax. The average Canadian pays more than half of his or her income in various kinds of taxes. Each year, somewhere around the middle of July, the media loves to tell us when the day finally comes "when you can start keeping your own money." *Before* that date — over halfway through each year — *every single penny is going to one government or another in some form of tax.* There is no denying that taxes have enormous effects on our lives. For this reason, it's crucial to consider the tax implications of your investment decisions.

We have no control over what taxes the government chooses to charge us. We do, nonetheless, have some control over the amount of tax we pay. And I am eager to help you avoid at least some of the potential tax hit on your finances — and legally, too!

Planning Is Key
Proposal for a simplified tax form:
    1. How much money did you make last year?
    2. Mail it in.

                    — Anonymous

Despite the modest proposals for tax reduction often made by our federal and provincial governments, for most Canadian families **income tax** remains the largest single annual cash outlay. It significantly erodes disposable income and the wealth of most families. By implementing a variety of tax-planning strategies, a family can minimize the effects of a potentially large tax burden and maximize personal wealth.

Tax-saving opportunities, contrary to public perception, are not just for the wealthy. *Dozens* of strategies for tax deferral and tax reduction are available to the average Canadian family. *Saving as much as possible from the taxman should be a key element of any financial plan.* Never think that the difference will be too small to be worth the trouble. Remember that regular investment, even of small amounts, can combine with compound growth to increase your wealth surprisingly quickly. Let us say, for example, that through careful tax planning you were able to save $1,000 every year. If you took that thousand dollars and invested it in the U.S. Stock Total Return Index (see my discussion of *index funds* in the first section, above, and in **Step 3**, below), then after 30 years at current rates of return, your $1,000 yearly savings would be worth *$509,611.* That's quite a bit of money to *not* have to give to our governments, especially if we don't have to! As that famous and brilliant writer, Anonymous, once said, "It isn't what you *earn* so much as what you save that counts in the long run."

In this, Step 2, I shall take you through the maze of tax planning slowly and surely, giving you the knowledge you need to make wise decisions in this most crucial area of your financial life. Part B covers family-related tax-planning strategies; Part C looks ahead to your retirement; Part D covers general tax-planning strategies for your investments; Part E offers strategic advice for the self-employed; and Parts F, G, H, I, J, K and L discuss the unpleasant but necessary subject of taxes related to death.

Money Solutions Paying Our Dues Highlights
- On average, Canadian workers pay over 50% of their income on different kinds of taxes.
- Income tax is the largest single cash outlay eroding disposable income and the wealth of most families.
- Tax-saving opportunities are not limited to the wealthy. There are dozens of ways to defer and reduce taxes, all of which are available to the average Canadian family.
- If you save even a modest amount a year in taxes and invest that sum in an index fund, those "small savings" could be worth a substantial sum in three decades!
- Six out of ten businesses pay little or no taxes in Canada.

B: FAMILY TAX PLANNING STRATEGIES

With proper planning, there are several ways your family can end up paying a lot less in taxes. This section will help to clarify and explain the various options that are open to you. Keep the tax breaks described below in mind, not just at tax time but throughout the year, and *you could save thousands of dollars* — dollars that you can put to excellent use by investing them according to the advice given in Step 3!

Tax Credits
Take full advantage of any **tax credits** available to you. A dollar in tax credit is actually worth *more* than a dollar. How is this possible? Tax credits are

subtracted from the amount of basic federal tax that you are required to pay. Since your provincial taxes and federal surtaxes are calculated based on these basic federal taxes, this means that each dollar of credit can actually save you as much as $1.50 or more in taxes. Not a bad deal, Mr. and Ms. Canadian!

Income Splitting

Income splitting can save you a great deal of money; and it's legal, too. It basically means that you can arrange your family affairs in such a way that the tax burden is divided up among the various family members so as to *reduce the amount of taxes that must be paid.* Here are some possible income-splitting strategies:

- Contribute to a spousal RRSP if your spouse is — is, or will be — in a lower marginal tax bracket when the funds are eventually withdrawn.
- Make gifts to children aged 18 and over. This will enable them to earn sufficient income to absorb their deductions and credits, and to pay for certain expenses that you would ordinarily pay out of your after-tax dollars.
- The higher-income spouse should pay most of the household expenses, so that the lower-income spouse can save; both can then invest more of their incomes.
- Invest your child's tax benefit payments in the child's name, because the attribution rules will not apply to income earned on these funds.
- Apply to share Canada Pension or Quebec Pension retirement pension payments with your spouse. This, too, can save you on your tax bill.

Charitable Donations

You can save yourself a *lot* of tax dollars as you support your favourite cause(s). Your tax or estate planning advisor can show you numerous ways in which charitable donations can become a win/win/win situation: for you, for the charity or charities you respect and want to support, and even for the government. Suppose that you support a battered women's shelter, for example; the money you donate will assist that worthy cause, lower the amount of tax you must pay, and make it less necessary for the government to donate its own funds.

Here are a couple of tips on how you can maximize the tax benefits of your charitable donations:

- If you typically make large charitable cash gifts, and also plan to sell securities and realize capital gains on these, consider **gifting** the securities instead, to reduce your taxes.
- You can reduce your taxes payable and generate funds for investments or debt reduction by borrowing money to increase your charitable donations.
- Maximize your tax credits by claiming all donations made by you and your spouse on one tax return, preferably the one sent in by the lower income earner.

Saving Through Schooling
Take the time to understand how **tuition and education credits** work, and take full advantage of the carry-forward provision. You can carry forward indefinitely any unused portion of a student's tuition credit until he or she has sufficient income. And 17% of thousands of dollars of tuition as a personal tax credit can save you a lot.

Medical Expenses
Combine claims for any **medical expenses** across the family. The spouse with the lower income should make the claim, so as to maximize the tax credits.

Pension Income Credit
If you or your spouse is aged 69 or over and you are not making use of your pension income credit, consider purchasing an annuity or RRIF. This will generate annual pension income. If your pension qualifies, you can save 17% of up to $1,000 in non-refundable tax credits.

Lower Taxes Through Politics
If you contribute to the campaign of a candidate for election to the House of Commons, or to one of the registered federal political parties, you are

eligible for a **political contribution credit** of up to $500. The credit available is 75% of the first $200 in contributions, plus 50% of the next $350 donated, plus 33⅓% of contributions in excess of $550. The maximum credit is reached with a donation of $1,075. I *cannot* guarantee that your MP will not cross the aisle and join another federal party, however!

Buying a Home with Tax-Sheltered Funds

The **Home Buyers' Plan** permits first-time home buyers to borrow up to $20,000 from an RRSP without suffering tax withholding if the money is used to finance the purchase of a home. (You are considered a first-time home buyer if neither you nor your spouse has owned a home or lived in one as your principal place of residence in any of the five calendar years preceding the date of the withdrawal.)

If you withdraw funds from your RRSP under this plan, you must purchase a home by October 1 of the year following the year of withdrawal. The withdrawn funds must be repaid to your RRSP over a period that does not exceed 15 years. This 15-year repayment period begins in the second calendar year after the withdrawal of the funds.

Tax-Free Schooling

The **Lifelong Learning Plan** works in a similar way, but to fund educational opportunities. It allows you to withdraw up to $20,000 from your RRSP, on a tax-free basis, to finance full-time education or training for yourself or your spouse. A maximum of $10,000 can be withdrawn annually. RRSP withdrawals under this plan are generally repayable, in equal installments, over a ten-year period, with the first repayment due no later than 60 days after the fifth year following the first withdrawal.

Child Tax Benefits

Under the **child tax benefit system**, a base benefit and **a national child benefit supplement** are available to help lower-income families with children. Those who meet the income test are eligible to receive a nontaxable payment for each child under the age of 18. If you deposit a child tax benefit in a bank account, or invest it, in the name of the child, the income it earns will be taxed as the child's. The child tax benefit is eliminated for families with one or two children once family income reaches approximately $70,000.

Money Solutions Family Tax Planning Highlights

- Tax credits are there to save you money. Take advantage of *any* that you are eligible for.
- Income splitting — dividing your income among family members so that your tax burden is as low as possible — can lead to significant savings.
- Making donations to charities can save a lot of money in taxes, and do good at the same time.
- Leveraging your charitable donations can save you a lot of taxes.
- Take full advantage of tuition and education credit carry-forward opportunities.
- Combine the medical expenses of all family members and have the lower income producer submit the claim for them.
- Other tax credits available include pension income credits, political contribution credits, and the child tax benefit and supplement.
- The Home Buyers' Plan and Lifelong Learning Plan allow you to use some of the tax-sheltered money from your RRSP to fund the major expenses of buying a house or getting further education.

C: RRSP AND RETIREMENT PLANNING STRATEGIES

Old age is like a plane flying through a storm.
Once you are aboard there is nothing you can do.

— GOLDA MEIR, FORMER PRIME MINISTER OF ISRAEL, 1898–1978

With all due respect to the late Ms. Meir, I must disagree with the above statement. There may be nothing you can do about actually getting older, but there is *plenty* you can do to make the process more comfortable, starting with good financial planning for the so-called golden years.

An RRSP is one of the most effective tax-planning vehicles available today, under our current income tax structure in Canada. It is one of the few remaining methods by which you can prevent the government from taking more than it has to. In this section, I show you how to use your RRSP *not only* as an effective retirement planning vehicle, but also as a terrific *year-round* tax-planning tool. As we discussed in the RRSP entry in the first section of this book, the key to getting the greatest benefit out of your RRSP is to think of it not simply as a **retirement** vehicle, but as a registered savings plan, and potentially a very fine one.

Timing of Contributions

You may deduct from this year's taxes any RRSP contributions made during the year (minus any that were counted toward the previous year), or up to 60 days after the end of the calendar year, subject to your annual limit (see below). Generally, it is advisable to make your RRSP contribution as early as possible, to take advantage of tax-free compounding. Financial planning is like comedy: *timing is everything.* As I have noted elsewhere, if you invest the year's RRSP contributions in March of one year, and claim that deduction the following April, you can gain over 13 months' worth of returns from your investment. If you wait till the last minute, like the vast majority of Canadians, making most or all of your contribution for each year in the *following* February, you can waste a fortune of potential earnings.

Deduction Limits

Your RRSP **deduction limit** is the maximum amount of tax-deductible contributions that you may make in any one year. Your deduction limit is typically 18% of your earned income for the previous year, up to the following maximums:

> $16,500 in 2005;
> $18,000 in 2006;
> $19,000 in 2007;
> $20,000 in 2008;
> $21,000 in 2009;
> $22,000 in 2010.

After 2010, the dollar limit will increase in line with annual changes in the Average Wage — a measure compiled by Statistics Canada.

Your **earned income** for the purpose of determining RRSP contribution limits generally includes all of the following:

- employment income, as shown on your T4 or T4A;
- net rental income; and
- alimony and maintenance payments.

You can **carry forward** unused RRSP "room" from previous years. For example, if your RRSP deduction limit in 2005 was $16,500, but you made a contribution of, say, only $10,000, you will be allowed to make an additional deductible RRSP contribution of $6,500 in a future year. This provision can come in very handy should you land a windfall, inherit money, land a new job with increased pay, etc. Generally, you can carry forward excess contribution room indefinitely until you reach the age of 69, when your RRSP must be collapsed.

Any contributions made to your RRSP in excess of your deduction limit for the year are considered to be **overcontributions.** Under the current rules, if the total RRSP overcontributions exceed $2,000, the excess is subject to a 1% per month penalty tax. That's a *lot*, so consider yourself warned.

Additional Contributions

Retiring allowances that are received from your employer, either upon ordinary retirement, out of a retirement compensation arrangement, or for a loss of office or employment, can be transferred to your RRSP. The maximum transferrable amount is as follows:

- $2,000 for each full or partial year, prior to 1996, during which you were employed by a company that was paying the retirement allowance; plus
- $1,500 for each full year prior to 1989 for which employer contributions to a registered pension plan (RPP) or deferred profit-sharing plan (DPSP) have not vested.
- Lump-sum amounts received out of an RPP or DPSP may also be transferred directly to an RRSP.

Transferring Between Plans

If you wish to change the investments in your RRSP, or change the plan issuer, you can transfer your plan without triggering any taxes. However, you must be careful not to deregister the plan during the transfer process.

Withdrawal of Funds before Retirement

As discussed above, you can use an RRSP as a tax-planning tool that goes well beyond retirement planning, because funds from your plan can be withdrawn at any time. The reason for the withdrawal will determine whether you must pay taxes or not.

Here is a summary of these scenarios:

RRSP WITHDRAWAL SCENARIOS

REASON FOR WITHDRAWAL	TAX SITUATION
To buy your first home	No tax payable (see the previous section for details of the Home Buyers' Plan)
To pay tuition fees	No tax payable (see above for details of the Lifelong Learning Plan)
Maturity	Depends on what you choose to do (see "When Your RRSP Matures," with the "collapsed" RRSP below)
Cash	Amount withdrawn fully taxed as income

If you make cash withdrawals before the plan matures for a purpose other than those allowed under the Home Buyers' Plan or the Lifelong Learning Plan, the amount withdrawn is taxable as income. The financial institution is required to withhold a portion of it to submit to the government directly; how much depends on the amount withdrawn and on where you live (it is higher in Quebec than in the rest of the country), as follows:

AMOUNT WITHDRAWN	PERCENTAGE WITHHELD	
	Other Than Quebec	Quebec
$5,000 or less 10%	10%	25%
$5,001– $15,000	20%	33%
$15,001+	30%	38%

When Your RRSP Matures

Your RRSP **matures** at the end of the year that you reach the age of 69. This means that you must collapse it and move the funds to some other vehicle. Note that the deadline for final contributions is *December 31* of the year that you reach that age, not the end of February of the following year.

Note that *you do not have to wait* until your plan matures after your 69th birthday to withdraw funds from your RRSP and take advantage of the maturity options described below.

Your main options for making good use of the funds from your collapsed RRSP in your remaining years are outlined below (these options are also discussed in more detail in the Annuity and RRIF entries, in the first section of this book).

- A **fixed-term annuity** provides benefits to the age of 90, or, if your spouse is younger than you, and you so elect, until your spouse reaches that age. It may provide fixed or fluctuating income.
- A **life annuity** provides benefits during your life, or during the lives of you and your spouse. It may provide either fixed or fluctuating income. There may be a guaranteed payout option.
- A **registered retirement income fund** (RRIF) is essentially a continuation of your RRSP, except that you must start withdrawing at least a given minimum amount each year. This can provide you with a retirement income from the investment of the funds accumulated in your matured RRSP.

Money Solutions RRSPs and Retirement Planning Highlights

- The timing of RRSP contributions can make a huge difference in how much money you can save — and earn.
- Be aware of your RRSP deduction limit, and beware of overcontributions, as they can be costly. Remember, however, that you can carry forward unused room for many, many years.
- Additional RRSP contributions can be transferred to your own plan.
- RRSPs can be transferred from one institution or investment vehicle to another without triggering taxes.

• Funds can be withdrawn before retirement for several reasons and maintain their tax-sheltered status.
• When your RRSP matures (or even before), your main options for turning it into income for your golden years are annuities and RRIFS.

D: TAX PLANNING STRATEGIES FOR INVESTORS

One of the biggest mistakes people make when it comes to investing is to ignore the tax consequences of their decisions. In my discussion of bonds, below, I shall show examples of how taxes and inflation can wipe out all of the gains on your investments, and even leave you with a net loss.

If you are serious about getting real returns from your investments, I beg you to please pay attention, and ask lots of questions about the impact of taxes on your investment returns. Remember, *it is not what you make, but what you keep, that truly counts.*

In this section of Step 2, I help you explore the world of tax planning for your investments. I'll address some of the most frequently asked questions, and show you how to come out ahead of the game.

Interest Income
Any interest that you make from savings accounts, guaranteed investment certificates, bonds, treasury bills, or mortgages is fully taxable, just like your regular income from employment. Whether you received this income, or have left it to grow in the investment, you are responsible for including in your income tax any interest earned in the current year. Interest-bearing securities are typically the worst investments. This is because, after adjusting your gains for taxes and inflation, your returns can be as low as zero — or can even venture into negative territory.

Dividend Income
Dividends get preferential tax treatment. Thus, they're much more attractive than interest income. Your non-refundable federal dividend tax credit, combined with the effect of that credit on your provincial taxes, will result in a combined tax credit of approximately 25% of the dividend received.

Capital Gains And Losses

When you sell an investment, you incur a **capital gain or loss** equal to the difference between the **adjusted cost base** and the **net proceeds received.** Under current federal budget proposals, you must include in your income 50% of your capital gains for the year, net of capital losses.

Probably the most attractive thing about capital gains income is that *if you do not sell your investments, you pay no tax whatsoever.* Interest-bearing investments, on the other hand, pay their returns in the form of annual taxable income. If you are serious about maximizing your after-tax returns on your investments — and why wouldn't you be? — then your best strategy is to *invest for capital gains* by buying stocks, equity mutual funds, and index funds, and avoid interest-bearing investments, to reduce the amount you must share your returns with the federal government.

Capital Gains Reserves

This is a way to help defer taxes on major capital gains. If you sell capital property and take back a mortgage or note receivable from the purchaser, you may be able to claim a **capital gains reserve** for the proceeds, not due until a later date.

However, in most cases, you must include the taxable capital gain in your income over a period of five years, at the rate of 20% of the capital gain each year.

Loss Carry-Overs

If your allowable capital losses for the year exceed your taxable capital gains, you can apply them against capital gains of other years. You may carry allowable losses backward up to three years, or forward indefinitely.

Allowable Business Investment Losses (ABIL)

If you suffer a loss on a business investment, you may be able to claim an **allowable business investment loss (ABIL)** , which can reduce your income for tax purposes. In fact, although capital losses can be used only to reduce capital gains, 66⅔% of an ABIL can be used to reduce your total income from all sources.

Therefore, if you are a shareholder, or a creditor of a financially unstable private corporation, consider selling your shares, or debt, to an unrelated person before December 31 to realize an ABIL.

Capital Gains Exemption

Shares in a qualified small business corporation and qualified farm property still qualify for a $500,000 **lifetime capital gains exemption.** (This exemption was universal only a few years ago.)

If you plan to use your exemption this year, and you have outstanding **Cumulative Net Investment Lost** (CNIL) as of December 31, you cannot claim the full exemption. If you are a shareholder of a private corporation, the quickest way to reduce your CNIL is to increase your investment income, in particular, the interest or dividend income you receive from the corporation. I strongly recommend that you consult with a qualified tax expert for advice on how to use this strategy.

Investment Holding Companies (IHCS)

If you own a large investment portfolio, consider forming an **investment holding company** (this is what Warren Buffett did with Berkshire Hathaway). There are a number of benefits, including the following:

- income and capital gains splitting;
- planning for probate fees;
- sheltering assets from U.S. estate tax;
- creating earned income for the purposes of RRSP contributions;
- reducing personal net income to preserve certain tax credits and social benefits; and
- converting what might otherwise be non-deductible interest into tax-deductible interest.

There are also some drawbacks to investment holding companies, however. I strongly recommend that you get help from a qualified tax professional before embarking on one.

TAX PAYABLE AT TOP MARGINAL TAX RATES (%)

	British Columbia	Alberta	Saskatchewan	Manitoba
Capital Gains	21.85%	19.50%	22.00%	23.20%
Dividends	31.58%	24.08%	28.33%	35.08%
Other Income	43.70%	39.00%	44.00%	46.40%

	Ontario	Quebec	New Brunswick	Nova Scotia
Capital Gains	23.20%	23.11%	23.42%	24.13%
Dividends	31.34%	32.81%	37.26%	33.06%
Other Income	46.41%	48.22%	46.84%	48.25%

	Prince Edward Island	Newfoundland	Yukon	Northwest Territories
Capital Gains	23.69%	24.32%	21.20%	21.53%
Dividends	31.96%	37.32%	28.64%	29.65%
Other Income	47.37%	48.64%	42.40%	43.05%

	Nunavut
Capital Gains	20.25%
Dividends	28.96%
Other Income	40.50%

Money Solutions Tax Planning For Investors Highlights

• Taxes can have a significant effect on the returns you receive from your investments.

• Interest income from guaranteed investment certificates, bonds, treasury bills, and mortgages are taxable at the same rate as employment income, while dividend income from Canadian corporations is taxed at a lower rate.

• Only 50% of your capital gains for the year must be included in your income, net of capital losses. But if you don't sell your assets, you pay no capital gains tax.

• Other possibilities for saving taxes on capital gains include capital gain reserve, carrying over capital losses, and capital gain exemptions.

• If you hold shares or debt instruments from a corporation in unstable condition, consider selling them to claim an Allowable Business Investment Loss (ABIL).

• Investment holding companies can be powerful ways to diminish the amount of taxes you must pay; consult an expert before going that route, however.

• Careful planning of your investment strategies, and asking your advisor lots of thoughtful questions, could well mean a lot more money in your pocket — and in the pockets of your spouse, your children, and your descendants.

E: TAX PLANNING STRATEGIES FOR THE SELF-EMPLOYED

If you own your own business, you want to be sure that the tax-planning side of your business is bringing you maximum benefits. In this section, I cover many of the important issues, but I strongly recommend that you obtain guidance from a qualified, trusted tax professional if you are self-employed. All accountants are **not** created equal!

Incorporation

There are many benefits to **incorporating** your business. From a legal point of view, the potential for liability for a corporation is limited to assets owned by the corporation. Your personal property is protected. From a personal point of view, many people find that separating business and personal activities results in a more efficient operation. Incorporating a business also makes it easier for it to continue after the owner's death.

The major tax benefit of incorporating is tax deferral, obtained by qualifying to pay taxes at a reduced rate: 18% to 22%, which is much lower than what a salaried employee has deducted from each paycheque.

Shareholders' Agreements

If your corporation has more than one shareholder, be sure to establish a **shareholders' agreement.** This document can protect your rights as a shareholder, minimize disputes, and ensure a smooth transition in the event of a shareholder dying or choosing to withdraw from the partnership.

Corporate Loans

If you borrow money from your corporation, ensure that the loan is repaid by the end of the taxation year following the year in which the loan was taken. If you don't, the amount of the loan may end up included in your income and taxed at the personal rate.

Additional Tips

Here are some more assorted tax-planning tips for the self-employed.

- Pay yourself enough salary or bonuses, if you can, so that your earned income entitles you to the maximum RRSP deduction each year.
- Accrue any bonuses to reduce your corporate income to the small-business deduction limit, which is generally $200,000.
- Remember that accrued bonuses must be paid out within 179 days of the corporation's year-end.
- Pay yourself enough salary or bonuses to reduce the minimum tax liability.
- If you think that your CNIL balance will affect your ability to claim your remaining capital gains exemption, pay yourself dividends rather than salary.
- To obtain a tax-free return of paid-up capital, pay down shareholder advances as an alternative to taking an income.
- Consider retaining in your corporation any income that is eligible for the small-business deduction of $200,000; this will result in a welcome deferral of taxes.
- Consider employing your spouse and/or children, to take advantage of income-splitting opportunities.

There are plenty of other ways that the self-employed can realize huge savings through careful tax planning. Consult a trusted, qualified tax professional!

Money Solutions Tax Planning For Self-Employed Highlights
   • **Incorporating your business provides numerous and attractive tax benefits.**
   • **A shareholders' agreement can protect your rights, minimize disputes, and much more.**
   • **Loans from your corporation must be repaid by the end of the taxation year.**

F: DEATH AND TAXES

Nothing can be said to be certain except death and taxes.

— BENJAMIN FRANKLIN, AMERICAN POLITICIAN AND INVESTOR

Hundreds of years later, it's still hard to argue with Ben Franklin. (Though Milton Berle once responded that the inevitability of death and taxes wouldn't be *so* bad, except that, unfortunately, they don't come along *in that order.*) Since death is a sure thing, there is no excuse for not planning for it. As the excellent Canadian tax expert Evelyn Jacks puts it,

> *Not only is death inevitable, but it has significant tax implications that we can plan for while living. . . . Should you die, your property must be distributed to your beneficiaries, income up to the date of death must be reported on the final tax return . . . and CRA [Canada Revenue Agency, formerly Revenue Canada] must issue a clearance certificate to close your tax-filing account.*

In other words, to be cynical for a moment, our hearts may stop beating, but our wallets can still be emptied by our friends in Ottawa. In a way, it's only fair: our RRSPS or RRIFS have been growing steadily; we may have property that has gone up considerably in value over the years; we have very possibly created a portfolio outside an RRSP that has grown greatly over the years and decades — so the government can hardly be blamed for not wanting to lose out on its share.

Can I Avoid Taxes Upon My Death?

If you can't escape the Angel of Death, can you *at least* avoid the greedy hands of Ottawa? Certainly not entirely. But if you take care to learn something about income-tax laws *before* you die (it's certainly easier to do that than to learn it afterwards!), then your foresight can very well reduce the amount of taxes due, and even avoid some taxes altogether through charitable giving and other means (see my comments on Estate Planning, below, for more details).

In other words, engaging in a little tax planning before you leave this earth can ensure that you leave quite a bit more money in your RRSP, RRIF, and the rest of your estate for your beloved spouse, children, or other beneficiaries. Not for nothing did our grandparents tell us, "A stitch in time saves nine." Putting time into sewing a few stitches now, *before* your passing, could make the Government of Canada a less wealthy beneficiary of your estate.

As I have noted elsewhere (for example, in the entry on Capital Gains in the first section), your home is exempt from capital gains. This means that you can leave it to the beneficiary of your choice *without* being hit by any taxes whatsoever. What a relief!

I am also happy to report that any treasury bills or guaranteed investment certificates in your estate will be only *grazed* by taxes, since any money owed will be based on the interest earned in the year of your death alone.

Sadly, *your RRSP* will be mugged, cut up, and left for dead, unless you make a very thoughtful spousal transfer before you die. How serious can this hit be? Well, if the value of your RRSP is $1,000,000, and you are in the top marginal tax bracket, your loving widow(er) could sadly see $500,000 being sent down the Trans-Canada Highway to Ottawa.

If you name your spouse as beneficiary to your RRSP — or your RRIF, if you have already collapsed the former into the latter — then these harsh taxes will be deferred until your spouse joins you in eternity. If you leave certain other assets to your spouse as well, you can ensure that they too receive "favourable tax treatment." Assets that have grown *outside* registered plans can be legally "rolled over" to your spouse upon your death, with all capital gains taxes untouched until he or she cashes them in, or passes away as well.

Make no mistake: these taxes will *eventually* come down hard on someone. It need not be the spouse of the deceased, who will not only be in mourning but very possibly fearful of his or her financial future. But one day the eventual beneficiaries — child, grandchild, or sibling — will see the taxman's blade come down. It's nice to know, however, that this action can be made to occur later rather than sooner.

Why God Invented Accountants

I must emphasize that these tax consequences are not easily explained, nor are they particularly clear. As one respected accountant, Lionel W. Newton, wrote in the *Estates, Trusts & Pensions Journal* a few short years ago,

> *The Income Tax Act rivals the Internet in the complexity of its interwoven parts. . . . Its subsections spin an intricate web that must be traversed carefully in order to determine the tax consequences when a taxpayer dies owning a registered retirement savings plan.*

In other words, as Mr. Science used to warn on those children's TV shows, ***"Don't try this at home, kids!"***

A Few Things You Should Know

Still, there are a few key points you should understand yourself. After all, the better informed you are, the better able you'll be to plan.

- A spouse may continue to contribute to the RRSP of the deceased, providing that it was a spousal one, and there was unused RRSP contribution room. The surviving spouse must be under the age of 70, and the money must be deposited during the year of the owner's death. Keep this possibility in mind; this investment could undergo strong compound growth over the years ahead.
- RRSPs and RRIFs that have *not* been left to a spouse are considered to have been cashed in, and are taxed heavily.

• Any property aside from the principal residence, together with any other assets invested outside a government-registered plan that are not left to a spouse, are considered to have been sold at "fair market value" at the time of your death. This is called a "deemed disposition," and if capital gains are judged to have occurred, it could result in a large tax hit on the final return of the deceased.

• The very act of naming beneficiaries has powerful tax implications and can be a superior tool in tax planning:

• If assets with little or no capital gains are left to siblings or children, and other assets with large capital gains to the spouse, very little tax (possibly none!) will be due.

• Never forget that if a spouse (or common-law spouse) is named beneficiary, all RRSP and/or RRIF assets can be passed over to him or her *with no immediate tax due.* These can be transferred into the spouse's own plan, or a new one can be created. With wise tax planning, the registered funds can continue to compound and grow tax-deferred, without affecting the widow(er)'s own RRSP contribution limit.

• Don't forget about the flip side of capital gains: capital losses. Keep accurate and clear records of any of these losses that have occurred; they can be applied against the often-large capital gains left to survivors.

• Estate taxes could come into play for Canadians who own property in the United States. A "non-resident alien" can expect to be hit with U.S. estate taxes if his or her spouse dies owning over $600,000 U.S. in property. There is an unfortunate chance of these assets being double-taxed, i.e., getting hit by both Ottawa *and* Washington. There are, however, numerous strategies available to reduce any potential U.S. estate taxes.

Some Final Advice

"The wages of sin are death, but by the time taxes are taken out, it's just sort of a tired feeling."

— *Paula Poundstone, American comic*

It may seem unfair, even farcical, to think that taxes continue after one's death. (This fact recalls a witty line from the 1960s Beatles hit "Tax Man," which warns that even the pennies left on your eyes in the coffin may be taken away.) It seems cruel, too, that a survivor must worry about the deceased's tax-filing deadlines, pension receipts, Canadian Pension Plan death benefits, investment income, capital assets, RRSP and RRIF accumulations, proceeds and transfers, GST credits, and more at a time when he or she will be concerned primarily with grieving for the loss of a spouse, parent or sibling. But we don't really expect life to be fair at this point, do we? The reasonable response is for us not to grumble (well, not *too* much), but to do some tax planning before we die, so that much more of what we have earned and invested over the years will end up in the hands of our loved ones, and less of it in the hands of Ottawa bureaucrats.

Sandra E. Foster's excellent book *You Can't Take It With You* is highly recommended; so is *Evelyn Jacks on Tax Savings*. Death is obviously unavoidable. It's good to know, however, that many of the taxes that follow it can be postponed, reduced, or even avoided all together.

Money Solutions Death and Taxes Highlights

• **Death has major tax implications, which you should plan for while still alive.**

• **Foresight can reduce the amount of many taxes, and even eliminate others.**

• **With planning, you can avoid your RRSP being slashed by up to 50% in taxes after your death.**

• **You can save your estate considerable money through a few simple acts of foresight, such as naming beneficiaries for your RRSP and property astutely; keeping track of any capital losses you have incurred; and being aware of potential tax hits on property owned in the United States.**

G: ESTATE PLANNING

A story is told about the brilliant Polish-born pianist Arthur Rubinstein
[1886-1982], who was one of the world's greatest interpreters of Chopin.
He once marched into a restaurant to join some friends, and began
to apologize. "So sorry to be late. For two hours I have been at my
lawyer's, making a testament. What a nuisance, this business of a testament.
One figures, one schemes, one arranges, and in the end — what?
It is practically impossible to leave anything for yourself!"

— FROM THE *LITTLE BROWN BOOK OF ANECDOTES*

It's a common misconception that estate planning is only for the wealthy.
The fault may lie in the dual meaning of the word "estate"; I mean it in the
sense of "a dead person's collective assets and liabilities," but of course it is
often also used to refer to a rich or costly home, as in "the Bill Gates estate in
suburban Seattle, Washington." The truth is that estate planning is an exercise you should go through whether your "estate" consists of the assets of Bill
Gates, or merely a modest RRSP and a tiny home with a large mortgage.

A lot of people — including some financial "experts" — mistakenly
believe that estate planning is an exercise to protect your assets only after
you are dead. *Not so.* If you plan for your estate properly, you can manage
your assets a lot more effectively while you are still alive — and have a lot
more left over to bestow upon your beneficiaries after you pass away.

What Should Be in an Estate Plan?
From Canada's foremost authorities on the subject come several solid suggestions on how a good estate plan. . . .

> • ensures that your executors, beneficiaries, and trustees will
> not have to guess at your wishes or intentions once you're
> gone;
> • provides control — it provides those who live on after you
> with the control over your estate they will need to maximize its
> value;
> • protects your beneficiaries — it ensures a consistent standard

of living and provides for the financial needs of your surviving spouse, dependants or heirs;
• protects your capital — good estate planning minimizes probate fees, income tax (on moneys received by your beneficiaries), capital gains tax, and legal and administration fees (associated with managing your estate after your demise), all of which can really eat into your assets;
• maximizes tax protection — so you don't pay more in taxes after death than you paid in income tax over your lifetime;
• ensures business succession planning according to your desires — the only sure way that you can see to the survival and prosperity of your business in the afterlife is by planning for it now; prevents unintended distributions — an estate plan should make sure that the people or institutions get the assets you want them to get — and that others, such as a prior spouse or specific relatives — do not receive certain assets or, in fact, anything, should this be your desire; and
• maximizes liquidity for survivors — you may be gone, but they will live on and have to pay for your funeral as well as ongoing expenses of your estate, such as mortgage payments on property until it's sold.

I always feel saddened when I recall that barely 4 in 10 Canadians over the age of 45 or so, do proper estate planning. Some 6 out of 10 middle-aged citizens of this country are very possibly going to leave their spouses, children, and grandchildren in confusion and possible despair, as the taxman digs far deeper into their legacies than should have been necessary had they only chosen to plan for their eventual demise.

Your First Step in the Estate Planning Process
Depending on the size and complexity of your estate, you may need to work with an investment advisor, an insurance advisor, a tax accountant, and an estate planning lawyer. Each of these professionals brings a unique discipline and expertise to your estate planning process.

Try not to be daunted by the thought of bringing all of these experts to the table. Consult any one of the above advisors with whom you have a good working relationship and ask his or her opinion about who should be involved in the planning process.

It is worth repeating that *no one individual* has all of the expertise you need to prepare and implement an effective estate plan. Your investment advisor will advise you on the most effective way to structure your investment portfolio. Your insurance advisor will help you purchase the right fund and the cheapest life insurance. Your tax accountant will structure your affairs so as to minimize the taxes your estate will have to pay. And your estate planning lawyer will help with such issues as family and succession laws.

In most cases, hiring these professionals is well worth the expense. They could save you many times their fees in tax reductions, reduced probate fees, reduced insurance premiums, and increased rates of return on your investments. Indeed, you should be prepared to consult this team and update your estate plan as many times as necessary over the years. When your circumstances change, your estate plan must address those changes.

Some of the events that could require changes to your estate plan are:

- marriage (or re-marriage);
- divorce;
- a death in your family;
- the birth of a child;
- retirement;
- the sale of your business, or your equity stake in the business; and
- an inheritance.

An Estate Planning Checklist
The following checklist will help you determine where you stand with regard to your estate plan:

- Have you completed a will?
- Have you completed a financial power of attorney?
- Have you completed a personal-care power of attorney?
- Are these documents up to date?
- Have you named beneficiaries for your RRSPs, annuities, life insurance policies, RRIFs, and pension plans?

• Have you carefully considered having one or more back-up executors, and have you followed up with the necessary steps?
• Have you given adequate thought to the allocation of your assets for your dependants?
• Have you done what you can to ensure that conflicts do not arise among your dependants?
• Did you make adequate allowance for income-tax liabilities?
• Are your assets properly registered to minimize income taxes and facilitate rollover to your spouse or qualified dependants?
• Do you have a living will?
• Have you made proper plans for charitable giving?
• Are your records organized in such a way that your dependants and executors can gain easy access to them?
• Do you review and update your estate plan as circumstances change?

Woody Allen once joked, "I don't want to become immortal through my work. I want to become immortal through not dying." This great one-liner makes us laugh because it acknowledges two powerful facts in our lives: that we all must die, and that we all struggle to avoid confronting that inevitable event. But *we mustn't let our desire not to think about an unpleasant subject keep us from acting responsibly.* Estate planning — writing a will, naming an executor, and all the associated time-consuming, sometimes costly, but essential actions — will free our loved ones to remember us with love and gratitude, rather than with disappointment that, through childish denial of death, we left them an ugly financial mess to clean up after we are gone.

The rest of Step 2 will introduce you to the important issues involved in estate planning and help you get started. Now, to look at wills, the role of the executor, the questions of probate, trusts, power of attorney, and why you should be thinking about all these topics — sooner rather than later.

Money Solutions Estate Planning Highlights
• Estate planning is *not only* for the wealthy!
• A good estate plan should cover everything from protecting capital for beneficiaries to maximizing liquidity for survivors.
• Have you prepared and signed a will? Does your family know the

names of your professional advisors and where your financial records and insurance policies are? If you can answer "yes" to these and a few dozen other vital estate planning questions, you could save thousands. Make sure you've taken care of all the important aspects; Sandra Foster's checklist is a good place to start.

H: WILLS

The family sat around the huge wooden table in the lawyer's office in
breathless anticipation as he read the will. "To my wife of 55 years,
I leave the house, the cottage, and $20-million," intoned the lawyer
solemnly. "To my faithful servant Max, who served me wonderfully for
over a quarter century, I leave $100,000. To my business partner Johnny,
I leave the entire factory and my best wishes. And to my nephew-once-
removed, Herbie, who has been begging me every year for forty years
to 'remember me in your will' — HELLO THERE, HERBIE!*"*

— OLD JOKE, AND A GREAT ONE

A will is nothing more (or less) than a legal document that details the manner in which you intend your assets to be distributed after your death. It allows for your beneficiaries to receive their legacies in a timely, orderly, and efficient manner.

What If I Don't Leave a Will?
A lot of things that you *would not* have wanted to happen, trust me.

But in one sense, *everyone* has a will. If you never took the time and trouble to prepare your own, then you'll get the one that has been written for you by your friendly (if not particularly-knowledgeable-about-your-desires) government. Since you probably will not want faceless bureaucrats deciding who gets your assets and who will take care of your minor children in the event of the untimely death of both their parents, then it's a very good idea to make sure you have a will created by *you*.

Dying without having prepared your own will is called **dying intestate**. As you can imagine, there are many ramifications when this occurs.

Asset Distribution

If you die intestate, your assets will be distributed according to your province's intestacy rules. There is no flexibility to these rules; as a result, the people you want to benefit may be left out, and those who do benefit may not be the ones you would have chosen.

The following chart outlines the distribution rules across Canada as of May 31, 2001, the latest available. The "preferential share" is an amount distributed to the spouse after debts are paid but before any other calculations are made.

Province	Preferential Share	Spouse + 1 Child Remaining Assets	Spouse + 2 Children Remaining Assets
British Columbia	$65,000	1/2 to spouse 1/2 to child	1/3 to spouse 1/3 to each child
Alberta	$40,000	1/2 to spouse 1/2 to child	1/3 to spouse 1/3 to each child
Saskatchewan	$100,000	1/2 to spouse 1/2 to child	1/3 to spouse 1/3 to each child
Manitoba	$50,000	1/2 to spouse 1/2 to child	1/2 to spouse 1/4 to each child
Ontario	$200,000	1/3 to spouse 2/3 to child	1/3 to spouse 1/3 to each child
Quebec	nil	1/3 to spouse 2/3 to child	1/3 to spouse 1/3 to each child
New Brunswick	nil	1/2 to spouse 1/2 to child	1/3 to spouse 1/3 to each child
P.E.I.	$50,000	1/2 to spouse 1/2 to child	1/3 to spouse 1/3 to each child
Nova Scotia	$50,000	1/2 to spouse 1/2 to child	1/3 to spouse 1/3 to each child
Newfoundland	nil	1/2 to spouse 1/2 to child	1/3 to spouse 1/3 to each child

Province	Preferential Share	Spouse + 1 Child Remaining Assets	Spouse +2 Children Remaining Assets
Northwest Territories	$50,000	1/2 to spouse 1/2 to child	1/3 to spouse 1/3 to each child
Yukon	nil	1/2 to spouse 1/2 to child	1/3 to spouse 1/3 to each child

If you have not made a will, no one can manage the affairs of your estate until an administrator is appointed by the government. This administrator is given powers similar to that of an executor to administer your estate. Everything will be held in limbo until he or she has been appointed. Ask yourself: *do you want your family, or beneficiaries, to be subjected to such hardships that may arise because of this delay?*

Administration Costs

This government-appointed administrator will, of course, need to be paid — out of your estate. If you have appointed your own executor in your will, you can determine a payment agreement. Leaving the matter to the government leads inevitably to higher costs. The few hundred dollars it may cost to prepare a will could end up being a small price to pay, considering the many thousands of dollars that a government-appointed administrator might charge your estate.

Income Tax

Your final tax bill might end up being a lot larger than it should be if you neglect to leave a will, and to do proper estate planning. Your government-appointed administrator will simply follow the "letter of the law" and dispose of assets as he or she sees fit to meet the requirements for any tax liabilities your estate may have. He or she will not necessarily act in the best interests of your beneficiaries. What a waste of hard-earned funds, potential for compound interest, and thoughtful investing!

Guardianship of Minor Children

If both parents die intestate, the government will appoint a guardian for any surviving children under 18. As a parent, this is something that I would certainly not want to see happen to my own children. The government — not your beloved sister, not your loving parents — will decide who should be named as guardian to take responsibility for the raising of your children. You do not need to be a student of classic fairy tales to know how easily this could turn into a tragedy for your offspring. Surely the loss of their parent or parents is horrible enough!

What Should Be in a Will?

Assuming I have convinced you *(I have, haven't I?)* of the importance of leaving a will, you'll be wondering next what should be in it.

A will need not be a lengthy, complex document. It should clearly state the intentions of its author in words that can be easily understood and acted upon by those responsible for administering the estate. A confusing will — and there have been countless ones through history — can be worse than no will at all.

What you say in the will is mostly, of course, up to you. Its purpose is to express your desires. But there are a few key clauses that every decent will should have, as follows:

• **Identification** — The will identifies who you are and your place of residence. It also states that this is your "last will," which means that any previous ones (such as the one which provided for an earlier, now-divorced spouse, or a sibling who no longer needs your assistance) are revoked.

• **Appointment of executor(s)** — You must name one or more individual(s) or an institution as your executor.

• **Payment of taxes, debts, and any fees** — This clause instructs your executor to pay any debts (such as loans, funeral expenses, mortgages, etc.) out of your estate, and authorizes the payment of any income taxes or probate fees that may be due.

• **Specific bequests and legacies** — This is where you detail the distribution of personal property to loved ones, and the bequest of specific cash amounts.

• **Guardian appointments** — If you have children under the age of majority, name a guardian for them in your will.

• **Attestation** — State that you have read and understood the contents of your will, and that there were witnesses to your signing.

Depending on your estate and your wishes, you may of course want to include other clauses. A **life interest clause** bestows upon a beneficiary the use of an asset or its income, but not its ownership. Upon the death of this beneficiary, the asset will pass on to another person, whom you also identify in the will. You can establish **testamentary trusts** and set out their terms in the will. These can split income, manage assets for minors, and help save taxes. An **encroachment clause** grants a trustee the flexibility to give a beneficiary additional funds for particular needs that may arise.

A Few Famous Wills

It might be instructive, or at least amusing, to share at this point some stories of wills connected with well-known personages from history. Rabelais [1494-1553] was one of the most important authors in the history of France; his *Gargantua and Pantagruel* ranks among the great satiric works of all time. In his will, he purportedly declared, *"I owe much. I possess nothing. I give the rest to the poor."*

Cecil Rhodes [1853-1902], the British-born financier and eventual prime minister of the Cape Colony of South Africa, made huge fortunes in diamond and gold mining. When he died and his will set out the distribution of his vast wealth, it turned out that most of the money was directed toward the setting up of the Rhodes Scholarships, which continue to support brilliant young students around the world today. Rhodes's immediate family was reportedly resentful that he had given such enormous amounts to bright youth, yet so little to his siblings. "Well, there it is," said his brother Arthur. "It seems to me that I shall have to win a scholarship."

In the late 1600s, Ninon de Lenclos was a French woman whose salon attracted many prominent literary and political figures of the era. In her will, she left only ten *ecus* (just a few dollars) to provide for her own funeral, as she wanted it to be as simple as possible. However, she asked her attorney, Monsieur Arouet, if she might leave a thousand francs to his son, who was a clever young man studying at the time, so that he could purchase some books. The attorney's son grew up to be Voltaire, one of the greatest thinkers and authors of the millennium.

All these historical figures have one important thing in common: *They were wise enough to leave a will.* Even the impoverished Rabelais clearly understood that one's estate need not be grand to be worth providing for after one's passing.

I urge you to follow their example. If you are not sure how to structure your will, I urge you to get assistance from a trusted professional. A few hundred dollars in fees now could save your estate, and your loved ones, many times that amount when you are no longer among the living.

Money Solutions Wills Highlights
• A will is a legal document that details the process for distributing a person's assets in a timely, orderly, and efficient manner.
• Lack of a will can make the distribution of assets more difficult and more costly, and can cause considerable delay. A guardian could be named by the government to care for any surviving young children, if there is no will that names a guardian of the deceased parent's choice.
• Each province of Canada has its own intestacy rules for distributing the assets of those who did not leave proper wills.
• A quality will identifies its author, appoints executor(s), allows for the payment of taxes, debts, and fees, sets out the terms of trusts, and more.

I: THE ROLE OF THE EXECUTOR

Let's talk of graves, of worms, and epitaphs;
Make dust our paper, and with rainy eyes
Write sorrow on the bosom of the earth;
Let's choose executors and talk of wills.

— WILLIAM SHAKESPEARE, IN *KING RICHARD II*

An executor does not, in fact, execute prisoners, but rather, the wishes of the deceased. It refers to the person you name in your will to handle your estate after your death. An executor must be prepared to carry out a long list of tasks, prudently and promptly, to the satisfaction of all.

What Are The Executor's Responsibilities?
The primary job of an executor is to protect the deceased's property until all debts have been paid, and to distribute the remaining assets to the people who are entitled to them. The executor must follow the instructions in the deceased's will to the letter. As mentioned above, if there is no will, a court-appointed administrator will manage the deceased's estate according to the intestate law of the province.

Some of the other functions an executor must perform are outlined as follows:

- The executor starts the probate process.
- He or she decides whether or not it is legally permissible to transfer certain assets or items immediately to the people named to inherit them.
- He or she is responsible for finding the assets of the deceased person and managing them during the probate process. This may involve deciding whether to sell real estate or securities that are part of the estate.
- The executor handles day-to-day details of the estate, such as terminating leases and credit cards, and paying expenses still outstanding — utility bills, mortgages, outstanding phone and cable charges, etc.
- He or she may have to set up an estate bank account to hold money that is owed to the deceased.
- The executor invests proceeds of the estate as stipulated in the will. If no guidelines are given, then the executor makes investment decisions on behalf of the estate, within the laws of the province.
- He or she pays taxes on the estate. A **terminal tax return** must be filed, covering the period of time from the start of the tax year to the date of the death.
- The executor may borrow on behalf of the estate, if necessary.
- He she may consult other professionals as necessary and

ensure that they are paid for their services on behalf of the estate.

Choosing an Executor

As you can see, the executor has a great deal of responsibility. By naming him or her (or them) in your will, you can decide who will look after your estate on your behalf when you are gone.

You should select someone that you trust completely, and who has the financial and business wisdom and acumen to manage and distribute your assets. (For example, if you were a conservative, savings-bond-loving investor, you would probably not want a day-trader or penny-stock-lover to handle your estate!) Make sure that you choose someone who is willing to accept the job — ask first — and can handle the duties fairly and responsibly.

You can appoint more than one executor.

Your executor can be your spouse, but if you appoint your spouse it is recommended that you have a co-executor as well, in case something should happen to both you and your spouse at the same time.

Executor Compensation

Executors are entitled to compensation; the amount usually ranges between 3% and 5% of the value of the estate. With an estate worth millions, this can end up being a considerable amount of money. You can also negotiate with your executor (while you are still alive, of course!) and settle on a fee, which you should record in a written agreement.

Final Thoughts

Richard Brinsley Sheridan [1751-1816] was an Irish-born English playwright who wrote several of the finest and funniest comedies for the stage ever created, including *The Rivals* and *The School for Scandal*. He also was a member of the British Parliament for over 30 years. Interestingly, for all his success in art and life, he was perpetually short of cash, and his son Tom was likewise unsuccessful in handling money. Once, the father and son had a furious argument, and a few days later, Richard Sheridan told his son Tom that he had made his will, and cut him off with a shilling. *"I'm sorry to hear that, sir,"* declared the son. After a moment's thought, the son added, *"You don't happen to have the shilling about you now, do you?"*

Handing over that shilling, of course, was a job for Sheridan's executor. Your own executor's job is to execute your wishes as outlined in your will, within the framework of the law. It is up to you to make sure that you spell out these wishes — clearly. State *exactly* how you would like to see your estate handled, managed, and divided. Dwelling a little on this topic now, unpleasant though it may be, will ensure that your will — in both senses of the word — is carried out.

Money Solutions Role of the Executor Highlights
• Your executor is the person you name in your will to handle your estate after your death.
• The responsibilities of an executor include managing of the probate process, transferring assets to inheritors, taking care of the day-to-day details of the estate, paying taxes, and more.
• Executors are compensated by up to 5% of the value of the estate.

J: PROBATE

Whatever you have, spend less.

— SAMUEL JOHNSON [1709-84] ENGLISH WRITER

When you die, your executor will be given legal authority to deal with your estate. However, carrying out certain tasks — such as liquidating assets — requires the court to certify your will, showing that your executor is authorized to represent your estate. This process of obtaining court certification is known as **probate**.

The following assets are *not* included in the probate process:
• life insurance and, in most provinces, RRSPs and RRIFs for which you have named a beneficiary;
• assets registered in joint names, which will pass on to the survivor by right of survivorship; and
• any real estate you own outside of the province in which you reside.

Probate Fees

The cost of probate is generally based on the fair market value of all property that you own at the time of death.

As of Spring, 2006, probate fee schedules in Canada were as follows:

PROVINCE	PROBATE FEE SCHEDULE
Newfoundland	all estates − $80 for first $1000; $75 plus $5 on each $1000 thereafter
Nova Scotia	first $10,000 − $75 $10,000 to $100,000 − progressive to $820 over $100,000 − $820 plus 1.385% per $1000
Prince Edward Island	first $10,000 − $50 $10,001 to $100,000 − progressive to $400 over $100,000 − $400 plus $4 per $1000
New Brunswick	first $5,000 − $25 $5,001 to $20,000 − progressive to $100 over $20,000 − 0.5%
Quebec	notorial wills − no fee "English form" will−$65
Ontario	first $50,000 − 0.5% over $50,000 − 1.5%
Manitoba	first $5,000 − $25 $6 on each $1,000 over that
Saskatchewan	all estates − 0.7%
Alberta	under $10,000 − $25 increasing to $6,000 for estates of $1-million
British Columbia	first $10,000 − no fee $10,001 to $25,000 − $200 $25,001 to $50,000 − 0.6% over $50,000 − 1.4%
Northwest Territories	first $500 − $8 $501 to $1,000 − $15 over $1,000 − $15 plus 0.3%
Yukon	first $25,000 − no fee; over $25,000−$140

Minimizing Probate Fees

As you can see from the above chart, probate fees can quickly add up in some provinces. It is good to know that there are ways to cut down on these fees considerably, with some planning ahead.

• Arrange joint ownership. When you register ownership of any assets in joint tenancy with another person, and give them the right to survivorship, these assets will pass automatically to the surviving joint owner. Since these assets will not, therefore, form part of your estate, they will not be subjected to probate.

• Hold real estate outside the province. At the time of your death, any real estate that is owned by you outside of the province where you live will not be subjected to probate.

• Designate beneficiaries. If you have designated a beneficiary under the terms of your RRSP, RRIF, pension plan, annuity, or life insurance policy, those assets will pass directly to the beneficiary without becoming part of your estate. Here, too, you can avoid probate and probate fees.

• Have multiple wills. Probate fees are usually calculated on the value of your gross estate. This means that debts (with the exception of mortgages or other claims against the real estate) are not deducted when calculating the estate value. This can affect the value of your estate, as seen in the following example: If the gross value of your estate is $500,000 and your debt ($100,000 of which is your mortgage) is $300,000, then the net — after debt — is $200,000. But your probate fees will be based not on that $200,000 but on $400,000 — that is, on the difference between the gross value of your assets ($500,000) and your mortgage (of $100,000). *Multiple wills can eliminate this problem*. You can make out a primary will, which is used to deal with probatable assets, and a secondary will to deal with assets that require probate. There are drawbacks to having multiple wills, however. I strongly recommend that you spend a few hundred dollars to get good legal advice from a trusted professional estate lawyer on this topic.

• **"Gift"** assets *before* you die. You can reduce the value of your probate estate by making gifts while you are still alive. (This practice is affectionately known as "giving with a warm hand rather than with a cold one.") There is no gift tax payable in Canada, although there may well be income-tax consequences. The tax rules state that if you dispose of any property, whether by selling it or by giving it away, and there are no proceeds, or if the proceeds are less than the fair market value of the property, *you will be deemed to have received an amount equal to the fair market value of disposed property*. This means that if you give away assets, you may have to report capital gains on them. Do not ignore this fact.

• **Prepare a revocable living trust.** Like gifting assets to another person, this allows you to bypass your will and avoid probate fees by transferring assets into a trust. When assets are transferred to a trust for estate-planning purposes, the change in ownership triggers a taxable **deemed disposition**. This means that, for tax purposes, the assets are treated as if they were sold by you, and then purchased at fair market value by the trust. Income tax on deemed disposition of property can be delayed until your death, when the assets are paid out of the trust to your beneficiaries. No probate fees are payable on those assets.

A Final Word

Good planning can considerably reduce the amount of probate fees your estate has to pay when you die. However, be sure to do your probate planning in conjunction with other tax-planning strategies, and not on its own.

And, as always, hire a trusted professional if you feel one is needed.

Money Solutions Probate Highlights

• **Probate is the process of obtaining court certification by the executor authorized to represent your estate.**
• **Probate fees are calculated differently in each province and territory.**
• **You can avoid, or at least minimize, probate fees in several ways. These include arranging joint ownership of assets, designating beneficiaries, and drawing up multiple wills.**

K: TRUSTS

Trust your husband, adore your husband, and
get as much as you can in your own name.

— ADVICE TO COMIC JOAN RIVERS FROM HER MOTHER

A trust is a formal arrangement wherein the legal owner of assets or property (called the settlor) transfers them to the care of a **trustee**, who is appointed to manage them according to the rules of the **trust agreement** on behalf of the assets' ultimate beneficiaries. Thus, a trust has four components: Property, Settlor, Trustee, and Beneficiary.

Participants in a Trust
• **The settlor** is responsible for placing assets or property in the trust. He or she also sets up the rules for operating and winding up the trust.
• **The trustee** must carry out the instructions in the trust agreement and manage the assets in the trust. He or she is also responsible for filing income tax returns.
• **The beneficiaries** of the trust receive the benefits of the assets held in the trust. These benefits can be in the form of income or capital property.

Terms of a Trust
Canadian trust law is very flexible; you can create a trust very much as you like. The terms of a trust usually specify the following:

• the purpose of the trust;
• the assets to be put into the trust;
• how those assets will ultimately be distributed;
• the beneficiaries of the trust;
• the names of the trustees you are appointing;
• the powers granted to the trustees; and
• what benefits the beneficiaries will receive from the trust.

A trust is something that could last for many years, so I urge you to seek out the help of a qualified professional when setting one up, so as to avoid mistakes that could prove costly down the road.

Testamentary Trusts

In effect, your estate is a type of testamentary trust that receives its instructions from your will. Clauses in the will name the trustee, the beneficiaries, the assets to be held in the trust, and how they are to be managed and ultimately distributed.

The most common types of testamentary trusts are spousal trusts and family trusts. Let's look at each of these.

Spousal Trusts

A spousal trust can be used to hold all or a portion of your assets for the benefit of your spouse upon your death.

Your spouse would have exclusive rights to all of the income of the trust, and, where provided for in your will, the capital of the trust during his or her lifetime.

A spousal trust can be useful in several ways. It can
 • help you defer tax by avoiding deemed disposition at fair
   market value;
 • help you split income, which can save considerable money on taxes;
 • help minimize probate fees; and
 • provide for your children if you or your current spouse
   remarries.

Family Trusts

Family trusts can be used to reduce the tax burden on your immediate family.

On January 1, 2000, a new "kiddie tax" came into being in Canada, which prevents parents from diverting investment income to children under the age of 18 in order to save taxes. Not all was lost, however. Here are nine thoughtful strategies for family trusts, as outlined by the respected Canadian business journalist and chartered accountant Tim Cestnick:

1. Spouses and adult children — If the trust is established for the benefit of a spouse or kids who have reached age 18 in the year, the kiddie tax won't apply on income taxed in the hands of these beneficiaries.

2. **Second-generation income** — Don't underestimate the power of second-generation income — that is, income on income. Where the kiddie tax might apply to dividends, and certain other income, any subsequent income earned on these amounts won't face the tax. Even where the family trust has nothing to do with a private business (and therefore has no kiddie tax problem), the regular attribution rules can still apply to interest and dividends earned in the trust, but second-generation income will avoid the attribution rules. Be sure to keep a separate investment account for the second-generation income.

3. **Surtax savings** — A trust can still provide some relief from provincial surtaxes where the income allocated to the beneficiary out of the trust is at a level below the various thresholds where surtaxes kick in.

4. **Transferring capital gains** — If you own assets that you expect to appreciate in value in the future, it's possible to transfer those assets to a family trust, with minors as beneficiaries. Capital gains realized in the future on those assets can be taxed in the hands of the beneficiaries without fear of the kiddie tax or attribution rules. One caution: there will be a deemed disposition at fair market value when assets are transferred to a trust, so count the cost of any tax hit first.

5. **Splitting interest income** — The new kiddie tax doesn't apply to interest income at all. You can lend money to a family trust, charge interest at the government's prescribed rate (6% at the time of writing), and avoid all attribution — and the kiddie tax. Any income earned on the funds loaned to the trust in excess of the interest charged will be taxed in the beneficiary's hands.

6. **Multiplying exemptions** — A family trust is still a great tool to multiply certain tax exemptions. Two exemptions in particular come to mind: the enhanced capital gains exemption and the principal residence exemption. For example, if the family trust owns shares of a small private corporation, it may be possible to utilize the $500,000 capital gains exemption of each beneficiary. Similarly, if the trust owns a home, it may be possible to use the principal residence exemptions of each adult beneficiary to shelter any gain on sale from tax.

7. **Financing an education** — The family trust can serve as a flexible education saving tool. The key is to avoid, as much as possible, the kiddie

tax and the attribution rules on income in the trust. This can be done by focusing on capital gains, and by reinvesting second-generation income. Once the minor beneficiary reaches age 18, the kiddie tax and attribution rules won't apply. In conjunction with an RESP, the family trust can make for tax-efficient education savings.

8. **Disabled children** — Where there is a child in the family who is mentally infirm, a family trust is critical. After all, it's important to ensure that an infirm child will be looked after once his or her parents are gone. The trustees in this case will be responsible for the financial well-being of the child. A family trust can also be used to preserve government benefits being paid for the benefit of the child, whereas a direct gift of assets to the child could reduce the amount of those government benefits.

9. **Estate planning** — Don't forget about the estate-planning benefits of establishing a family trust. The new kiddie tax won't affect the use of a trust for creditor-proofing, business succession planning, probate-fee reduction, minimizing taxes on death, and avoiding compulsory succession schemes.

Inter Vivos Trusts

No, this is not a disease. Sometimes called **a living trust**, an **inter vivos trust** is one created during the settlor's lifetime. Inter vivos trusts can be useful in the following ways:

- to protect assets from creditors;
- to minimize probate fees;
- to minimize the income taxes due on death, by freezing the value of investments or the shares of a business;
- to provide one individual with the use of the property, with instructions to transfer the property to someone else after death;
- for charitable giving;
- to provide privacy for your beneficiaries, since trust assets do not become a matter of public record; and
- as an alternative to a power of attorney, since a trust agreement can provide more detail and control over how assets are to be administered.

Bearer Trusts

If you have set up an account at the bank or opened an investment account for a child under the age of 18, you may have registered it as something like "David Smith, in trust for Kendal Smith" (David being the father and Kendal the daughter). Any income, dividends, or capital gains on this account will be attributed to Kendal.

This type of set-up does not require a trust agreement, because it is not a formal trust. Legally, property in a bearer trust becomes the child's property when the child reaches the age of majority.

Money Solutions Trusts Highlights

- A trust is a formal arrangement wherein the settlor (the legal owner) transfers assets or property to a trust.
- A trust agreement specifies its purpose, what assets should be placed in it, who the beneficiaries are, and what powers are granted to trustees, among other things.
- The settlor has the responsibility of placing assets into the trust, and setting up the rules for operating it and eventually winding it up.
- The trustee follows the instructions in the trust agreement, files income tax returns, and manages assets in the trust.
- Beneficiaries of a trust receive the assets held in the trust, whether income or property.
- There are several different kinds of trusts, including testamentary trusts (the most common being spousal and family trusts), inter vivos trusts, and bearer trusts.
- There are many wise strategies for trusts. They can provide second-generation income, surtax savings, a way of transferring capital gains, an opportunity for interest-income splitting, a method of financing an education, estate-planning benefits, and more.
- It is strongly recommended that you obtain help from trusted professionals in the areas of tax and estate planning if you want to establish a trust.

L: POWER OF ATTORNEY

Thine is the kingdom, and the power, and the glory.

— MATTHEW 6:13

Most of us simply love to tell one another anti-lawyer jokes. But a "power of attorney" need *not* involve a lawyer at all. **A power of attorney** grants authority to make decisions about your finances, and possibly even your property, to someone else if you become physically or mentally incapacitated.

While power of attorney is considered part of estate planning, it concerns the care of your estate before, not after, your demise. It is not morbid, just realistic, to acknowledge that hundreds of thousands of people every year have strokes, are knocked down by cars, have heart attacks, and fall ill for weeks and even months. These situations are not necessarily linked to advanced age, and — this is important — are *not* covered by a will you may have written (see **Wills**, above).

You can see the difference at once: your will grants an executor authority to act on behalf of you and your beneficiaries after you are dead; a power of attorney (in Quebec, it's called a **mandatory**) provides the power to a spouse, family member, or dear friend to make decisions on your behalf while you are still very much alive.

Arranging for power of attorney is a crucial part of estate planning, even for those who have very little money or property, and even for those who are still young and vigorous. Think of the fine actor Christopher Reeve, of Superman fame. One awkward step by a horse, one brief fall at a bad angle, led to a painful life and an early death in a wheelchair, hooked up to a breathing apparatus for most of his last few years.

This kind of sudden occurrence is a reality faced by many thousands of men, women, and children every year.

What Kind of Power?

So, what can the person to whom you grant power of attorney do? This power is like most decisions in life in that it can be broad or restricted, general or limited. (Imagine loaning your car to your newly licensed teenager with the warning to "have it back in that garage before midnight." That would be a restricted, or limited, use of the vehicle.) One simple but common example: if you winter in the Caribbean, you may wish to have a dear friend pay your bills while you are gone. In such a case you are not ill; you are still competent; but you plan to be out of the country for a while, and wish to keep your credit rating good. So you grant someone you trust the authority to perform certain specified tasks on your behalf for a limited period of time.

A broad power of attorney, on the other hand, could give your designated person free rein over all your affairs, even including the sale of property (this might be equivalent to letting the kid keep the car all summer long). A limited power of attorney might specifically exclude authority over certain investments, or particular aspects of your finances ("Don't touch those bonds," perhaps).

In short, the person to whom you grant this power can do as much or as little as you are willing to "hand over," except for one thing: *he or she may not touch your will.* Other than that, we assume you would only grant this power to someone extremely competent and trustworthy, not the sort who would spend your money lavishly or unload your property in ways you would never have accepted if you were available and in perfect emotional, physical, and mental health.

Any power of attorney you grant vanishes upon your death, of course; its entire purpose is to make sure that your affairs are cared for in the ways you would desire while you are incapacitated, but still alive. Rules regulating power of attorney vary quite a bit from province to province — for example, a power of attorney document must be registered in a courthouse in some provinces, while others demand two witnesses at the signing — so be sure you know the regulations in your own place of residence.

A Living Will

A power of attorney document may also include a **living will**. Sometimes called an **advance health-care directive**, this outlines your wishes concerning artificial means of extending your life. Such a document does not always have full legal status, depending on the province, though it is generally considered to be *morally binding* by family and medical personnel.

The kind of situation calling for a living will is something most of us would prefer not to think about, but it can be an important part of any estate planning. Consider the following questions for a moment, painful as they may be:

- What if you were in some kind of serious accident? Would you want "extraordinary measures" used to resuscitate you?
- What kind of care do you want arranged if you begin to slide into irreversible Alzheimer's disease?
- If you were suffering from an excruciatingly painful ailment, would you want to put a limit on how long you would accept life support?

The examples, alas, are endless — as are the moral, ethical, and religious implications. I do not propose to tackle such challenging questions here. Rather, I recommend that you think about what your own wishes are, and create a living will of *some* kind, in a separate document, at the same time as you write up a power of attorney statement. Give copies of both to your family and a few close friends. These loved ones may bless you some time in the future for making sure they know your true wishes about how you want your medical care to be handled.

A Sample Power of Attorney Document

There are excellent, low-priced software programs available for creating living wills and other similar documents, and that a good lawyer might charge a very nominal fee to assist you with one. Nonetheless, I present you here with an idea of how a simple power of attorney statement might look; just remember that the exact requirements depend on your province's rules.

I, (YOUR NAME), of (CITY AND PROVINCE), a (YOUR PROFESSIONAL DESIGNATION), here appoint (NAME OF YOUR TRUSTED FRIEND OR RELATIVE) of (CITY AND PROVINCE), to be my attorney, and to perform on my behalf anything that I can lawfully do myself.

This power of attorney may be exercised during any legal incapacity on my part (or WHEN I AM IN FLORIDA, EACH DECEMBER THROUGH FEBRUARY, ETC.).

I am satisfied that the authority conferred on the attorney here named in this power of attorney document is able to provide effective management of all (OR PART) of my estate, in case I should become incompetent in any mental or physical manner.

In such an event, I direct that the person named in the power of attorney retain this power for the managing of my estate (OR, ONLY THE WRITING OF MY CHEQUES) during the time of my incapacitation.
Signed on (DATE)

And so on. As you can see, this document is far more painful to *think* about than it is to *create*. But the granting of a power of attorney and the creation of a living will could also grant peace of mind to your loved ones in a difficult time — a peace that may prove invaluable, in every sense of the word. Naturally, it would be wise to show your power of attorney document to a lawyer before you sign it, and to verify that it will stand up to any legal challenge in your particular province.

Final Thoughts

Andy Rooney, the witty and often profound essayist of *60 Minutes* fame, once noted, "Death is just a distant rumour to the young."

How true. When one is young, one understandably assumes that he or she will live forever. (Why else would kids smoke when they *know* what it's doing to them?) But even young people die, have horrible accidents, catch dreadful diseases.

Wise and thoughtful estate planning will never prevent our demise, alas. But following the suggestions on estate planning given throughout this section, at any age, could have a powerful effect on the financial and emotional well-being of our families and friends. Careful estate planning can make sure that the vast majority of the money you have earned (and invested and compounded) throughout your life will live forever, even if you cannot — and will end up in the hands of your loved ones, and not those of bureaucrats in Ottawa.

What better gift to leave them, along with fond memories and a lifetime of love and caring?

Money Solutions Power of Attorney Highlights

• Power of attorney is the authority to make decisions about your finances, possibly even your property, should you become physically or mentally incapacitated. You should grant it to someone you trust, by writing out a simple legal document, no matter what your age or wealth.

• Power of attorney differs from the role of an executor, who is granted authority by a will after you are dead.

• A power of attorney can be quite broad or very limited.

• As a wise citizen, you should create a living will to inform loved ones of your wishes regarding the use of extraordinary or artificial measures to resuscitate you or extend your life.

• A power of attorney document can be simple to create, either with a software kit or by writing a simple statement and having a lawyer check it. Remember, however, that rules differ from province to province.

STEP 3

LEARN HOW TO INVEST
SAFELY AND PROFITABLY

Warren Buffet, arguably the world's greatest investor, once said, *"There seems to be some perverse human characteristic that likes the idea to make easy things difficult."*

My goal has always been to show the public how *surprisingly simple* it is to create and follow a very successful investment strategy. One doesn't need to understand useless concepts such as market timing, forecasting, hedging, derivatives, mean reversion, portfolio optimization, risk adjustment returns, or standard deviation. All you need is *simple knowledge*, not a high IQ, to be able to invest wisely and successfully.

Accord to Buffet, there are two rules to follow, when it comes to investing: *Rule #1: Don't lose your money.* And *Rule #2: Don't forget rule #1*! Our education system has done a remarkably good job of taking simple things in life and making them complex. We all experienced this in our youth, especially in high school or university. Buffet, a student and friend of the great Benjamin Graham, the late, gifted scholar of value investing, once noted that Graham's theories are seldom included in college curricula today, because they "just aren't difficult enough"! Instead, schools teach far more complex, useless theories. The business schools, as well, reward *complex* behaviour over *simple* behaviour, even though simple behaviour is usually far more effective.

The investment industry — of which I have been a part for over a quarter-century — is also to blame. Over the years, we have seen, over and over again, how investment salespeople use complexity to confuse the public into believing that these money managers have some type of supernatural power to predict the future. Jack Trout, the author of *The Power of Simplicity*, put it best: "Everything we have learned in the Industrial Age has tended to create more and more complication. I think that more and more people are learning that you have to simplify, not complicate. **Simplicity is the ultimate sophistication**." I could not agree more.

The question is, how *do* you simplify the investment process? The answer starts with a concept that has been used for a long time, to deal with problems in our lives: if you, or someone you know, is addicted to drugs, alcohol or smoking; or if you, or someone you know, is obese, putting their health at risk, what is invariably the first step in solving the problem? It has always been to admit, "there is a problem." Admission, or confession, that a problem exists, is half the solution. Once there is that admission, then one can start to work on possible solutions.

The process of simplifying and creating an investment strategy that will give you a greater chance to succeed than the ones that are being used by most people today, starts with admitting, then, that you HAVE a problem. The problem — like addition to drugs or alcohol or fast food — is that *if you don't change what you are doing, it will destroy your life; in this case, destroy you financially*. Alcohol abuse, smoking and fatty foods are killing people, if admittedly slowly (but surely). However, the manufacturers of these products are getting richer and richer, aren't they!

The same thing is true of the way that most people's money is managed. The Money Managers (like the manufacturers of unhealthy products) are *also* getting richer and richer, and the consumers — you, and in the past, this writer — are getting poorer and poorer! Here are some very recent statistics, some of which I mentioned in my introduction and which are worth repeating, because they may shake your former beliefs:

• Altamira Investment Services, in early 2006, began offering a "High-Interest Cash Performer, paying 3.15% Daily Interest.

This may not impress you, until you realize that *this return is a lot better than the vast majority of "actively managed" mutual funds which you probably own!*

• In 2005, the number of Canadian Equity Funds (mutual funds which actively buy and sell — and "market time" stocks) that *beat* the Index (i.e., the TSX or Dow Jones Industrial Average, which goes up and down — usually up — every year) was only **26 — out of 266**! In other words, *less than 1 in 10 of these mutual funds beat the simple index!* Yet *mutual fund sales in 2005 hit $23.4 billion, the best since 2001,* believe it or not!

• *The average return of the five largest Canadian Money Market funds was 1.5%* — less than one-half what Altamira is now offering with their new "High-Interest Cash Performer"! And the amount of money that Canadians have placed in **these** miserably performing funds? *Nearly $15-billion!* And hundreds of thousands of trusting Canadian investors have been paying high expenses to the managers of these funds, to receive such awful results! (Even ING Direct was paying 2¾% on no-fee Savings Accounts during this time!)

• More shockers: *the average 5-year performance of Templeton Growth Fund, which is the largest mutual fund in Canada, has been 0.3%!* Meanwhile, the Royal Bank's **stock** price increased by 30% in 2005, as did the Bank of Montreal's and Toronto Dominion's! (During the year that RBC's stock shot up by nearly one-third, guess what it was offering on its "Signature Plus Account" in all of its banks — if your savings balance is less than $1,000? **Zero.** *No wonder* the Royal's stock price did so well!) (The Canadian Imperial Bank of Commerce [CIBC] was fined $2.40-billion during 2005 for "illegal trading," by the way).

Active vs. Passive Investing

Remember my opening statement in this Step about *Keeping It Simple*?

What on earth could be more simple than sitting PASSIVELY by, watching your earnings accrue, than ACTIVELY running after profits, like Javert chasing Jean Val Jean in *Les Miserables*, and failing most of the time?

Let me explain. A large majority of funds in Canada are "actively managed funds." All this means is, that professional money managers use a number of measures to assess potential investments. Problem: these actively managed funds usually take countless, unnecessary steps with your money, in the frustrating attempt to "time the market." (See my lengthier comments on this flawed concept in the opening section on financial terms.)

Scholars in the investment field keep proving the fact that active managers are unlikely to add any value to your investments, because the stock markets of the world are highly efficient; they will go up and down, and, as the old saying goes about the Wheel of Fortune, "where it stops, nobody knows." I've said it before in this book, but it is worth repeating, and memorizing: "It's not *timing* the market that matters; it is time *in* the market." So, despite the endless hoopla and millions of dollars spent plugging this mutual fund or that, it is next to impossible for the average investor in an **actively managed fund** to get the kind of returns that are regularly published in newspapers and magazines. (Think of those famous "fortune tellers" and "prognosticators" you see on TV now and then: sure, this one predicted Kennedy's assassination and that one predicted a Middle Eastern war breaking out. But these "geniuses" never mention their utterly wrong predictions, or the fact that they failed to foresee the tsunami in Thailand or Hurricane Katrina devastating the Gulf Coast of the U.S.)

Why is it that last year's hot mutual fund performers almost inevitably end up under-performing the following year? The answer lies in how the mutual fund firms play the game: a game that is guaranteed to make their companies win, and you, to lose.

Here is what happens: You (and millions of others) see these Great Performing Funds advertised and you (understandably) think to yourself, "Wow! I'd better put some of my money into these winners!" But if you do, you've just *broken* one of the cardinal rules in investing: *Don't buy high!* What is even worse, is that if your sales person wants to sell your "under-performing funds," in order to get you to switch to another fund, you've just committed the other major cardinal rule of investing: *you sold low!*

The mutual fund companies, in the meantime, are in a glorious, win-win, no-lose situation! Either way, they come out making money: They promote their high-performing funds for the next year (to keep the money coming in); they make their management fees on the new sale; and then they make *more* money, when you transfer out to other funds!

What, then, is the solution to this rather ridiculous situation you find yourself in, when you purchase actively managed funds?

The Simple Solution: A Passive Investment Strategy

Passive investing is another way of saying "INDEX INVESTING." And it makes total sense, and is as simple and sensible as breathing: a passive investment strategy allows you to invest in the securities/equities/stocks that are in the "index" that you choose — in the same proportion, so that the fund performance reflects the market performance. By "same proportion," I mean that, for example, if XYZ GOLD makes up 4% of the Toronto Stock Exchange Index (TSX), your purchase of an index fund based on the TSX will carry 4% of XYZ GOLD. The same goes for your purchase of the Dow Jones Industrials; if GREAT BIG CORP. makes up 7% of the total index of the New York Stock Exchange, that's the percentage your index fund based on the Dow Jones will carry of *that* company.

And What Do the Experts Say?

The more I read about Index Investing, the more I recognize how right the smartest experts are. Here is Ted Cadsby, in his book *The Power of Indexed Funds: "If you want to increase the odds of investing in a 'winner' and more importantly, reduce the odds of investing in a 'loser,' then indexing is the way to go."* I find it informative that *Fortune Magazine*, in an article published only days before the entire high-tech madness, along with Nasdaq, came down like a deck of cards (in mid-March, 2000), declared, *"Building a portfolio around indexed funds isn't really settling for average (or a little better). It's about refusing to believe in magic."* Now, I love magic as much as the next person, and I think that David Copperfield puts on a great show. But why believe in magic, when your very financial future — and those of your spouse and children — are at stake?

If authors and journalists aren't enough, then how is this: the words of a Professor of Economics at the University of Toronto, Eric Kirzner: *"Naturally, there are many critics, including a number of active fund managers, who present arguments against passive [index] investing. However, most of these arguments are spurious."* How true, professor. True, index-based investing has gained ever-wider acceptance among professional money managers, even if, for many individual investors, indexing is a relatively new concept. While most of my readers may have heard of indexing, or read about it in the business press (in other words, they've picked up some *information* but not *knowledge!*), investors may not always realize just *how compelling the case is for this mode of investing one's money successfully.*

What, Exactly, Is Indexing?

The index of a book tells us what's in it. So what's an index fund? The other term for it, "passive investing," gives you a good start toward understanding its power and glory. Indexing is simply an investment method that replicates — matches — the performance of a given market index. What too many people don't fully realize, however, is that there are many more hundreds of indexes (or indices) than the familiar Standard & Poor 500 or the TSX: one can buy "into" the index of whole sectors of an economy, such as Financial Sector in Canada, or the Energy Sector in the U.S., or the indexes of entire countries (!) such as Japan, South Korea, Mexico, Brazil, and, yes, even China (which a growing number of thinkers are insisting will soon own the 21st Century as much as the United States owned the 20th).

The strategy behind indexing is as powerful as it is uncomplicated. So, instead of actively researching and picking stocks — an exercise that fails consistently — and hoping and praying that this stock or that fund will outperform an index such as the NASDAQ, index managers buy and hold the same stocks that are represented in the various indexes, in the same proportions.

Here are some of the reasons why indexing should be the cornerstone of every intelligent and knowledgeable Canadian's investment strategy:

> • **Simplicity and transparency** — indexing strategies are transparent and totally unambiguous: what you see is, quite literally, what you get. Unlike the "AIM Dent Demographics Trends Class Fund" or the "CI B2B RRSP Fund," or — my personal favourite — the "CI Global Boomernomics Fund," an index fund allows you to focus your attention on, and dedicate your energy to, the risk/return trade-offs of different asset classes, instead of trying to second-guess the investing styles of many different mutual fund managers. I urge you to stop wasting your valuable time (and money) on the useless exercise of trying to

figure out the various styles of countless money managers, and listening to countless salespeople, whose appetite for commissions is invariably greater than their desire to do what is right for you, their client!

• **Lower fees** — It should not surprise you that *the lower fees charged by index funds actually translate into higher returns*! Active money managers incur higher commissions, higher management fees, and higher bid/ask-spread costs. One estimate suggests that *the trading costs for active portfolios are about six times greater than they are for passive investing.*

 One reason for lower fees with the index strategy is that index managers, by the very nature of their work, *do not need* the large staff of research analysts and portfolio managers that is inevitably required by actively traded funds. Have you ever wondered why you are paying — through overpriced management fees — to have analysts give you their favourite predictions (in other words, "wild guesses") — when they usually end up being as profound as the following insight: "There is a 50/50 chance that the market might go up." Thanks — but no thanks.

• **Tax efficiency** — Taxes are sometimes left out of the investing equation, but they are an essential part of determining your real return. *Investing in an index fund can significantly reduce taxes.* The next time your friendly, neighbourhood mutual salesperson tries to sell you a particular fund, make sure you inquire about the *tax implications* of that fund, and how its (probably frequent) buying and selling of stocks will affect the return you will receive.

• **Effective diversification** — With an indexing strategy, you can create a well-diversified portfolio of bonds, cash, stocks and more — and this diversification helps you to reduce risk. For example, if you want to diversify within your stock portfolio, you can choose among the major U.S. indexes, as I've noted — the Dow Jones, S&P 500, and so on, as well as the TSX 300 Composite Index and the TSX 60. And what could be more "diversifying" than *international indexes from major countries around the world*?!

• **Performance** — Study after study after study has shown that **indexing consistently outperforms active management** — which is, in many cases, merely a kind of "market timing with a college education."

Why Such a High Success Rate of Index Funds?

Investors pay too much in fees for active management, which cuts down on the amount of their eventual returns. (Compare as much as 8% over a year to manage *active* funds to as low as *one-half of 1%, even less,* for indexing. Talk about already improving your return on investment!)

Too much cash is held in most active fund portfolios, for which you could be paying as much as 3% in annual fees. (And to think that you used to complain that your bank was only paying you 1% to keep your deposits!) In their lunatic, unsuccessful attempts to "time the market," these active managers often pull their (your!) money out of stocks, and hold on to it as cash, like an old man still recovering from The Great Depression. But during this same time, *many* stocks in the index of many major stock markets and even countries are moving up!

No one has the ability to consistently predict what is going to happen in the market. It may leap 8% one day, and slide 2% a week for the next six in a row, and then go up 1% a day for a month, after that. Suffice it to say, over long periods of time, the "market" WILL go up — it always has, and it always will. But, admittedly, this rise will never be steady, or predictable. Just like individual stock prices will go up, then down, then up, and up, again. Welcome to the strange and even bizarre "Mr. Market," as value/investing guru Benjamin Graham used to wittily mock the world of stocks. Mr. Market may act a bit psychotic at times, but you can nearly always rely on him to do well, over time.

The only reason why stock prices go up or down at all is that someone wants to buy them and someone else wants, or is willing, to sell them. According to Warren Buffett, arguably the Greatest and Wisest Investor in History, you can never win if you are involved in a game of "the greater fool's theory." And those great fools are always out there, theorizing like crazy, and always happy to waste your money.
Ignore them all.

Increased foreign diversification — Many Canadian investors understandably wish to diversify their investments beyond our borders. But current rules for registered tax-deferred plans limit foreign content.

rrsp-eligible index funds, however, offer an alternative approach that provides real exposure to foreign market indexes, but that the government still accepts as Canadian content for tax purposes.

Indexing should certainly be a major part of any intelligent, knowledgeable investor's portfolio. It's as simple — yes, simple — as that.

Why ETFs Are The Smartest Way To Go

Welcome to the 21st Century **Solution** to the "Crisis in Money Management," which I have also been guilty of perpetuating, when I ran my giant financial planning firm Fortune Financial, and three of the best initials I've encountered in my life since I-O-U: ETF.

Exchange Traded Funds deserve a book of their own. In brief, they are merely an investment tool that reflects the performance of different sectors in the market. Like "**iunits**" and "**ishares**," or **index mutual funds**, ETFs match portfolios of broad-based indices. To put it simply (which is the central thought behind all of Step 3!): When you purchase a typical mutual fund, you are buying into a dozen or two choices of stocks, or bonds, into and out-of which, money managers are continually leaping (incurring charges, and taxes every time they make a move). When you purchase a single stock in a single firm, you are buying a tiny chunk of that one company. But *when you buy an ETF of the Stock Market Index of Mexico, say, or China, or Japan, or Canada, or the U.S., you are purchasing a broad section of every important share listed in those nations' major companies!* **Isn't that wise?**

Yet, for all the advantages, there are no real *dis*advantages in buying ETFs: units of ETFs trade on all stock exchanges; they can be bought and sold easily; they can be purchased on margin; their holdings are posted daily, so investors have full knowledge of each fund. (How many readers of this book know what individual stocks their favourite mutual fund is presently holding, and in what volume of each — and which that fund held a month ago, or what it will hold next month?) ETFs are **tax efficient, cost efficient, fully invested** (they don't need to hold cash, in anticipation of redemptions, like mutual funds must), and, best of all: **the MERs of ETFs — their "management expense ratios" — are invariably strikingly low:** sometimes as little as one-quarter of 1%! Fully managed (market-timed) mutual funds have MERS which can reach as high as 2.5%, which can deal a severe blow to your earnings each year, even when the mutual fund happens to do well.

Simple? Yes. But **brilliant**. I agree with Warren Buffet, who often has bragged that he "never invests in businesses he doesn't understand," which helped him avoid the dangerous high tech crash of 2000, and keeps him in "dull" and "boring" companies such as billion-dollar insurance firms, Dairy Queen, Coca-Cola, Gillette, and so on. Oh — and **he's** worth tens of billions. How is YOUR portfolio doing?

Now That I Know About ETFS, What Things Should I Be Investing *In* — And *Why*?

There are several different TYPES of INVESTMENTS which may interest you, and here is the good news: all of these, which I shall describe at length, below, have ETFS which use them as the basis of their content. So, if you've always had an interest in bonds, see the section on BONDS; and the same goes for MORTGAGES, PRECIOUS METALS, and all the other key places that you can place your money — and grow and grow and grow it. (Well, if you are wise enough to go the "passive" route, with segregated funds, or, my favourite, ETFS.)

Money Solutions Simple Investing Highlights

- Investing does not have to be difficult, convoluted, complex, or confusing in order to be successful. To be blunt, it can be surprisingly simple, and involve little jargon or obscure language.
- All the TV and radio shows and newspaper articles claim to have the "answers," but more often than not, their information and advice are wrong, and following it will only make it worse.
- It is the mutual fund firms that make the big bucks and the profits from most actively managed mutual funds, not the individual investor.
- Market timing is idiotic; investing in stock indexes is smart. Buying and holding a handful of quality stocks, which means owning a part of some great companies, is also smart. ETFS are nearly always the way to go.

A. BONDS

Government bonds were probably the first "financial thing" most of us were introduced to, after our weekly allowance from our parents. We were usually told — wrongly — that "Canada Savings Bonds are a very good investment." Well, Mom and Dad were right about how we should look both ways before crossing the street, at least.

Of course, there are many other kinds of bonds, in addition to those offered by federal, provincial, or municipal governments. Many companies sell bonds as well, known as **corporate bonds.**

To understand bonds, think of them as a sort of fancy "IOU," such as one you received from a university friend to whom you loaned a few hundred bucks in a pinch. When you buy a bond from a country or business, *you've loaned them money*, and *they must pay you back*. Your friend probably paid you back the same amount you loaned him, but one expects more from a government or a business, yes? So, you will get more, too: the issuer of the bond promises to pay you a certain rate of interest, along with the entire principal, or **face value**, of the bond, when it comes due — or **matures**.

Stocks vs. Bonds

The terms "stocks" and "bonds" are usually linked together, like peanut butter and jelly, or John and Yoko. Even though both are legitimate forms of investment, in many ways they couldn't be more different. A bond, by its very nature, must pay you interest of some kind. A stock, however, need not "return" a single penny to you, and often never does. True, there exist many great firms that have paid dividends on every share of their common stock, four times a year, for decades — but it's far more common to hear or read that "ABC LIMITED has suspended dividends this year," for various reasons.

A bond must repay that loan, or capital, of yours; you lent the government or business a certain amount of money, and you can justifiably expect to get it back. A stock never has to repay a single penny of the capital you put into it (although, naturally, you purchased it out of the hope that it *will* grow in value).

When you buy a bond, you retain control over your investment, and know exactly what its return will be. That may be important to some people. With stocks, you have no control over what will happen to its price; it depends on many things in the marketplace, and those often-illogical stock exchanges, which you cannot affect.

As you may have guessed by now, there is far more risk in purchasing a stock than there is in purchasing a bond. But there is also far, far, FAR more possibility of profit, even of riches, in buying stocks (which is really owning a tiny piece of a company) than buying bonds (which is really lending money to a company, city, province or country).

An Extraordinary Statistic

Here's an amazing stat that may well make your head spin, so we'll calm you down a bit by turning it into a little story about your grandparents:

> *Suppose that, in the mid-1920s, your grandparents on your father's side scraped together $10,000, and invested it in a variety of **quality bonds**. They left them to compound and grow over the next three-quarters of a century. You've just made the happy discovery of their purchases while going through some old family papers, and you redeem them.*
>
> *That original $10,000, invested in bonds, has turned into **$360,000**! Congratulations!*
>
> *Now, suppose that, also in the mid-1920s, your grandparents on your mother's side also managed to save $10,000. But they chose to invest it broadly across the market, purchasing **quality stocks** (equities) in good companies. You find the papers relating to this other 75-year-old investment in the same old box, and you cash it in, too.*
>
> *That original $10,000, invested in stocks, has turned into **$18-million**! We not only wish to congratulate you, but we want our children to marry into your suddenly wealthy family. Please consider our offer.*

Please do not misinterpret this little tale of your grandparents. Stocks have not *always* beaten bonds as investments. After all, the Great Depression murdered the stock markets of the world, and while many stocks/equities were crumbling into dust, most bonds continued to slowly but surely pay back the "lenders" who had bought those IOUs. There have been a dozen other times, over the past century, that bonds continued to pay on their promise, while the majority of stocks were taking a bath.

Yet you just saw what happened to the money invested by those wise grandparents who chose to "take the risk" and ride the often-lunatic volatility of the stock market. Their $18-million inheritance is a lot more than the $0.3-million you got from the *other* side of the family. Every known study has shown that, if you can tolerate the sometimes stomach-churning nature of the stock markets of the world, you — or your children or grandchildren — will inevitably end up far, far richer.

Academic Evidence

Had enough about fictional grandparents? Want some **real** scholarship? Here's some: in a recent study by the Society of Actuaries, some shocking facts emerged. A woman who is 65 today has more than a 1-in-2 chance of living to the age of 85, an over 1-in-3 chance of making it to 90, and better than a 1-in-7 chance of living until she is 95.

Good for her, you think. Her 65-year-old husband, meanwhile, has close to a 1-in-2 chance of living to 85, a nearly 1-in-4 chance of making it to 90, and a better than 1-in-13 chance of seeing his 95th birthday. Yes, it's true: women *do* live longer than men — but that is not the point that I'm trying to make, with these statistics.

The experts concluded from these numbers that, **when planning for your financial future, it is safest if you plan to "make it" into your 90s.** Yet if that 65-year-old couple invests their money in Government of Canada long-term bonds, *their chances of outliving their capital — and therefore finding themselves destitute — are very high*!

Two professors from York University, Kwok Ho and Chris Robinson, published a book in 2005 called *Personal Financial Planning*, which has some intriguing numbers in its appendices. Studying the "Average Returns of Different Investment Assets" over *nearly a full half-century* (from 1957 to 2004, to be exact), they looked at the "compounded average return" — without allowing for any money management fees (which can be huge in "actively managed funds") or income taxes.

Note the following numbers carefully: *A Canadian T-Bill averaged only 6.6% over those many years; Canadian Government Bonds, only 7.8%. The TSX Index, however, was up 9.7% over that period, and the S&P 500 was up 10.7%!* (And when the effect of inflation is taken into consideration — and who can avoid the savage claws of inflation? — *the Canadian T-Bill gave only a 2.3% average return, and the government bonds, a mere 3.4%. The two major indexes of the TSX and the S&P 500 were nearly double of each of those miserably low numbers*). The point? You may spend your last decade or two on this earth in abject poverty, if you don't look to ETFs and the indices of the world to invest in, since bonds are NOT the way to go — especially now that we're living so much longer than ever before in history.

In early 2006, when I was personally in touch with the impressive, award-winning Chris Robinson, Ph.D., CA, CFP, who is a Professor of Finance and Co-ordinator of Wealth Management Programs at the Atkinson School of Administrative Studies at York, he emailed me the following statement: "*A significant allocation to equity is important for most long-run situations, particularly retirement and planning long-term retirement. In the long-run, the short-term up and down swings of equity are more than compensated for, by the higher long-range average return, which most people will need to meet their goals.*" Then, the good professor added, kindly, "[Your] emphasis on ETFs squares with my own advice these days. Avoid all mutual funds in favour of them." It's nice to hear such agreement with my theories — and from a true expert and scholar in the field.

So, rather than becoming a "loaner" of your hard-earned dollars to governments or corporations by buying bonds, why not become an *owner* of some quality companies by buying equities? As Nick Murray, a prominent North American authority on investments, once wrote, ". . . bonds have historically had virtually no net return at all. The loaner set the world endurance record for treading water. Real wealth went to, and continues to abide with, the patient, disciplined, long-term owner. After inflation and taxes, the owner actually got paid five or six times what the loaner did." Wow.

The Deadly Duo: Enemies of Bonds
I have noted several times in this book that the wisest move for an investor is to buy and hold stocks or stock-related mutual funds — preferably index

funds or ETFs. But how does the buy-and-hold investor in bonds fare?

How does *JAMES* Bond fare, with all his enemies? Bonds have two major enemies, themselves: inflation and rising interest rates. Inflation, of course, is the enemy of *all* things: stocks, car prices, heating bills, university tuitions — *everything*. The reason why inflation is so brutal to the value of bonds is clear: it leads to higher prices, which means that a dollar tomorrow will purchase less than a dollar today. (A Volkswagen Bug cost about $2,000 U.S. in the mid-1960s; it's well over ten times that amount today.) Recall that bonds can lock up your money for as long as 10, 20, or even 30 years; and you can quickly recognize how inflation can slash away at the value they will have down the road, when they are finally redeemed.

But why interest rates? The standard rule goes like this: when interest rates change, the value of existing bonds moves in the opposite direction — by a ratio of 10 to 1. So, if interest rates drop 1%, the value of bonds goes up 10%. Sadly, if interest rates rise 1%, existing bonds go *down* 10%. So, if you earn 6% on a bond, and pay taxes of 2.4%, you have but 3.6% left. And if there is an inflation rate of nearly 4% (the average of the last two decades), your net earnings will be less than zero. Yes, after adjusting your gains for taxes and inflation, the return on your investment is actually *negative*, and you have *lost* money on your investment! Pretty shabby — like your clothes will soon look.

How To Invest in Bonds

If you *still* are interested in investing in bonds — after all I warned you about them! — there are several different ways of doing it. You can purchase them directly, which is the cheapest way. But to be successful in this, you must have large sums of money, and be able to speak the lingo: short-term notes, floating rates, book-entry bonds, bearer bonds, strip bonds, corporate bonds, and countless others. I believe that the average investor will be wise to stay away from this method.

Actively Managed Bond Mutual Funds

The mutual fund industry has done a terrible injustice to Canadians by misleading them into believing that bond mutual funds are a viable investment strategy. Peter Lynch, the brilliantly successful equity investor during the 1970s and 1980s, once said the following: *Their purpose in life eludes me.*

Bond funds have been consistently outperformed by individual bonds, some-times by as much as 2 percent a year . . . and doing worse the longer the funds are held." Two percent! Take a look at Step 5, below, about Compound Growth, and see how even a seemingly insignificant 1% difference in one's rate of return can make a huge difference in the long run.

Exchange-Traded Funds (ETFS)

This is probably your most efficient way to invest in bonds. There are several exchange-traded funds (ETFS) available in North America today:

On the TSX, there is iunits Canadian Bond Broad Market Index (XBB), and iunits Government of Canada 5-year Bond Fund (XGV).

On the AMEX, there are the following ishares: Lehman Aggregate Bond Fund (AGG), Lehman 1-3 Year Treasury Bond Fund (SHY), Lehman 7-10 Year Treasury bond Fund (IEF), Lehman 20+ Year Treasury Bond Fund (TLT) and TIPS Bond Fund (TIP).

Exchange-traded bond funds are purchased like stocks, and then (if you're smart), should be held in one's portfolio indefinitely for the interest they pay out each June and December. Like actual bonds, the prices of bond ETFS will fall precipitously if interest rates go up, but will rise if the opposite happens. But unlike bonds, these ETFS have no maturity date, so you are never sure that you will get your original investment back on a specific date. But who cares? If you approach bond ETFS in the same "buy and hold" fashion that wise *stock*holders do, you won't care about any dates of maturity and will simply keep receiving those interest payments until you choose to sell.

When it comes to fees, you pay only ¼%, which is stunningly low, compared to the over 2% charged by many bond mutual funds. Do you see now why no *rational* person should ever choose to invest in a bond mutual fund?

Money Solutions Bonds Highlights
- Buying a bond involves "lending" money to a company, city, or country, which must in turn pay you interest of some kind.
- Equities (stocks) always have a higher return than bonds over the long term. Period.
- Inflation and rising interest rates can brutally affect the value of bonds and their dividends.
- You can purchase bonds directly, or through mutual funds, but the

management fees of the latter will gobble up a large percentage of your potential return.

• You can also buy bonds through an index bond mutual fund, or through ETFS, which charge the lowest fees, therefore providing the highest returns.

• Do not loan your money to governments or companies through the purchase of their bonds. Rather, choose to own those companies by purchasing their stocks. Be an owner, not a loaner, and you'll end up better off.

B. GUARANTEED INVESTMENT CERTIFICATES

The name seems straightforward enough: **guaranteed investment certificate**. A GIC is a deposit certificate, usually issued by a bank, trust or insurance company. It requires a minimum investment and pays a predetermined rate of interest over a certain period of time. (The latter can be as short as 1 to 30 days or as long as five years.) But the words behind the initials "GIC" don't really tell it all. Oh, they are *guaranteed*, certainly. And they are, indeed, a kind of *certificate*. But an *investment*? Hardly.

Oh, GICs promise you security, alright. But as Helen Keller, that remarkable blind/deaf/mute woman once wrote, "Security is mostly a superstition. It does not exist in nature. Life is either a daring adventure or nothing." And *nothing* is close to what you get when you purchase GICs.

It breaks my heart that hundreds of thousands of retired people in Canada have tried to fund their older lifestyle with GICs which have often fallen precipitously over the years. Back in 1990, for example, an investor could opt for a five-year GIC paying 11.15%; within a half-dozen years, one could *not* purchase a *two*-year GIC that paid over 4.5% — a horrific decrease of income of well over 60%! When I think of the countless older citizens of our great country who depend on income from their GICs in order to make ends meet. . . .

Why, then, have GICs been so popular over the years? This question makes me think of that old song "Blame it on the Bossa Nova." I think we can probably blame this flawed investment's success on the Great Depression. After all, large numbers of our parents (or grandparents) suffered horribly through the nightmarish stock market crash of 1929, and the long, lean, hungry years that followed. Fearful of the risk involved in equity investments led to generations of Canadians turning to GICs.

Advantages and Disadvantages of GICs

There were some advantages, or so it seemed, since GICs always paid a higher rate of return than a bank account — often by a good margin. And the principal of a GIC — the money invested — never fluctuated in value, a reassuring feature to millions of Canadians. And they were so easily available! If you had some extra cash lying around, and were pretty sure that you wouldn't have to touch it for a year or two, then why not?

But there is a huge *downside* to GICs. You may earn a fairly decent return on a GIC, true, but most of it, as with a Canada Savings Bond, will be gobbled up by the feds in Ottawa. Indeed, the money you make on a GIC is taxed just like the salary you get each week from your place of employment: at the full marginal tax rate. (The only way to avoid this is to put your GIC within your RRSP, but why do this, when you can do so much better almost anywhere else? Unlike a bond fund, where you can yank out your money at a moment's notice without any penalty, a GIC may not be touched before it comes due — at least, without financial alarms going off. If you get hit with a catastrophic expense or family illness or whatever, you may have to pay a very large penalty; often it's as much as a half-year's worth of interest!)

The returns are still stunningly inferior to those possible almost anywhere else, especially in equities or equity mutual funds. Even a modest, uncontroversial, no-nonsense financial writer such as Monica Townson, in her *Independent Means — A Canadian Woman's Guide to Pensions and a Secure Financial Future*, headed her brief section on GICs with the summary: "Low Risk Low Return."

Index-Linked GICs

One relatively new product that is worth a closer look is the market-linked GIC, which is connected to a stock-market index. (And you *know* how I feel about index funds!) Banks boast that these offer the "potential to earn higher rates of return than with traditional GICs." And it's true: an index-linked GIC pays a guaranteed floor-interest rate, *plus* a possible increment tied to the performance of a particular market index, or a portfolio of market indices. The exact terms vary considerably, depending on the product and the seller. But like all GICs, they are always guaranteed.

Guaranteed — To Give You Low Returns

There are more and more products available involving this dull and usually disappointing investment vehicle: one-year cashables; five-in-one GICS (which divide the client's principal into five equal portions with varying maturity dates), and medical access GICS (which may be redeemable in whole or in part in case of a medical emergency.) But *however you dress them up, GICs give you only modest returns*. You would do *much* better in equities or equity mutual funds. Only with more knowledge — like I hope you are gaining from reading this book — can you escape the low-paying, high-taxed world of GICs.

True, GICs are not risky; there's no argument about that. And they are clearly guaranteed — indeed, they even come with welcome CDIC insurance when purchased from a bank or trust company. But I recommend that you stay away from them, in spite of the love for this guarantee held by your parents and grandparents, who may have feared "risking" their principal in the stock market. We know far better now, in the first decade of the 21st century, about how markets of the world act, than investors did back in the 1920s.

Money Solutions Guaranteed Investment Certificates Highlights

• Guaranteed investment certificates are usually issued by banks or insurance companies. They provide a predetermined rate of interest over a limited period of time.

• GICS are actually a very poor investment choice; they are usually purchased by people who live in fear of a repeat of the great stock-market crash of 1929 and the Depression that followed.

• GICS have major disadvantages, from being taxed at the full marginal rate, to not being liquid at a time of emergency. Yes, they are guaranteed, but they are low-paying and unsatisfactory as investment vehicles. They should be avoided.

C. MORTGAGES

A mortgage is a contract between two parties: one who wishes to *borrow* money (usually toward the purchase of a property), and one who wishes to *lend* money. The borrower is called the **mortgagor**; the lender, the **mortgagee**. In exchange for that money loaned, the borrower must provide some kind of security to the lender — usually in the form of a mortgage document to be filed against the property. The latter can be a house, a condominium, a duplex, even a plot of land. This contract is important, because in case the lender **defaults** on the loan — i.e., fails to make the agreed-upon payments — the lender, which is often a bank, can seize the property.

Advantages and Disadvantages
The advantages can be wonderful, as any proud homeowner knows very well: there is low risk, since real estate tends to appreciate in value. One can obtain a mortgage with very little initial cash (see my entry on Home Ownership and Mortgages in the first section of this book, above, and **Step 6, on Leveraging**, below). A mortgage can be a hedge against inflation, as the equity of a home builds up. And, of course, there can be real tax advantages; if you take out a mortgage against the value of your house and use that money to (wisely) invest in stocks or ETFs, the payments are tax-deductible.

The disadvantages of owning a mortgage can be troublesome, however. It lacks liquidity — meaning that you cannot sell a home overnight if you need money quickly. You must wait a long time to see any real return on your investment. There is always the risk of mortgage rates shooting up, if you are not locked in, possibly leaving you unable to make the payments — in which case you could lose the property.

Finally, there is the element of complexity; investing in a mortgage can demand quite a bit of study. There are so-called conventional mortgages, high-ratio mortgages, government-assisted mortgages, variable-rate mortgages, collateral mortgages, wraparound mortgages, secondary financing (second and third mortgages), discounted mortgages, leasehold mortgages, a builder's mortgage, a vendor's mortgage. . . .

As you see, taking out a mortgage is in no way like strolling into your neighbourhood bank or trust company to purchase a GIC!

Direct Investment in Mortgages

There are several ways of investing in mortgages. You can, of course, simply contract a mortgage yourself, and become a mortgagor. You can also take part in a limited partnership, forming an investment group in which a general partner bears the financial obligations and the day-to-day managing of the mortgage, while the other, limited, partners supply some of the capital. There can be serious disadvantages to the latter, which were discussed above, in the first section, on Limited Partnerships.

There are also indirect ways of investing in mortgages, some of which can be very attractive — if hardly the key to making huge sums of money.

Indirect Methods:
Mortgage-Backed Securities and Mortgage Mutual Funds

One **indirect method** of investment is through purchasing National Housing Act mortgage-backed securities (MBSS), which are administered through the Canada Mortgage and Housing Corporation (CMHC). These combine direct investment in an undivided interest of a pool of residential first mortgages, which are insured through the CMHC, with government bonds. These investment vehicles are considered comparable to top-quality government bonds in terms of risk, so you can breathe easily dealing with MBSS (our Government is behind them, after all); yet they have the potential for higher yields (i.e., returns on your investment) because of the mortgage component.

Since the mortgages are insured for the full amount of both principal and interest, no mortgage default can threaten your investment. You will receive your government-guaranteed payment on the 15th of every month. Your pool may include as many as a hundred residential mortgages, although there are other types of pools available as well. There also exist mortgage mutual funds, designed to provide a good level of interest income, while preserving your capital. The fund manager (who charges you a fee, of course), invests in mortgages of various types. Some funds include both commercial and residential properties; others hold only insured, government-guaranteed first mortgages on residential properties alone.

Still others invest indirectly in mortgages, through **mortgage-backed securities**, which consist of pools of mortgages that distribute their income — after expenses — to the holders of the securities. With these securities, you receive a payment every single month, consisting of your share of the month's interest on those mortgages and some of the principal. In a way, you become a banker making a loan to several home buyers. These indirect methods of investing in mortgages lack the major, often frightful, disadvantage of direct investment in individual mortgages, because there is never any collection problem. And they can offset the often frightening price volatility that is common in many other kinds of investments.

But there are disadvantages. Chief among them is the simple fact that, because of all the guarantees, you will never, ever come *close* to approaching the far larger rates of returns that invariably come (over the long term) from investments in Canadian or foreign equities, either directly purchased or in mutual funds. Mortgage funds of all kinds provide a higher level of interest income than do bonds, GICs, or treasury bills, and they are suitable for people who want or need interest income right away, or for those who desire a quality, conservative investment toward their eventual retirement. (Nearly all mortgage mutual funds are available for inclusion in an RRSP, and they can compound decently over the years.)

Naturally, because mortgage rates vary, so will the value of any mutual funds that invest in them, and of mortgage-backed securities. Returns will therefore fluctuate. And because they have a lower risk factor than equities and bonds (inside or outside of mutual funds), they will never deliver as large a return. Still, one particularly attractive aspect about mortgage mutual funds is that capital gains distributions are not very common, because mortgage fund managers have far fewer opportunities trading than do equities managers. So, if you want to avoid unnecessary capital gains at the end of each year, you may well wish to consider this solid, quite safe, if not very exciting (and not extremely profitable) way to invest in mortgages.

Money Solutions Mortgages Highlights

- There are advantages to investing in mortgages, including low risk and the small amount of money needed for the investment. It can be a hedge against inflation, and the investment can have real tax advantages.
- There are disadvantages to owning a mortgage as well: a lack of liquidity; the ever-present risk of increases in mortgage rates; even the loss of the property.
- There are various indirect ways to invest in mortgages, including

limited partnerships, MBSs, and mortgage mutual funds.

• There are some favourable arguments for these indirect ways of investing in mortgages, but one's return from any of them will never approach the much higher rates of returns available from investing in stocks, or in purchasing equity or index mutual funds.

D. GOLD AND OTHER PRECIOUS METALS

A Platinum credit card. An opportunity handed to you on a silver platter. A golden opportunity; a golden parachute; as good as gold. Clearly, precious metals have played a major role in our thinking, and in many of our economies, since ancient times. Peter L. Bernstein, brilliant investment dealer, scholar of risk management, and quality author, writes in his best-selling *The Power of Gold: The History of an Obsession*:

> [P]eople have become intoxicated, obsessed, haunted, humbled, and exalted over pieces of metal called gold. Gold has motivated entire societies, torn economies to shreds, determined the fate of kings and emperors, inspired the most beautiful works of art, provoked horrible acts by one people against another, and driven men to endure intense hardship in the hope of finding instant wealth and annihilating uncertainty.

What's so special about these shiny metals? Much of their attraction for investors is the fact that they cannot be debased and undercut by governments, the way currency can be. Throughout history, governments have often merely printed millions and even billions of paper dollars, leading to terrible inflation and the devaluing of their currencies, in order to pay off their towering debts.

Gold, on the other hand, is durable. Historians have noted with fascination that all the gold ever mined in history is still available, in shipwrecks on sea bottoms or in museums or in Fort Knox, yet all of it could be fit into any one of today's giant oil tankers; its total weight is a mere 125,000 tons! Compare that with over 120 *million* tons of steel produced every year! Ahhh — but is it worth investing in?

Pros and Cons of Precious Metals as Investments

It's a lot easier to find disadvantages to *investing* in gold, than it is to find gold itself. Remember the Bre-X scandal? It was one of hundreds of scams and frauds associated with precious-metal mining over the decades. Then, there is the cost of mining gold, which is extremely high. It can cost $300 and more to mine merely a single ounce of gold, meaning that the going rate must be quite a bit higher to make any project worthwhile — especially in northern Quebec or in the jungles of South America.

Gold has been called "a very silly investment" by one business writer, who noted that "it is highly volatile and very speculative." Just compare gold with a good stock in a quality company: the latter may grow in value and split several times, whereas one ounce of gold will always remain exactly one ounce of gold — and it will never pay dividends or interest, as many a good equity will. On the other hand, the arguments in favour of purchasing gold and other precious metals are hardly absurd. Gold, especially, can be a superb hedge against inflation, and when inflation runs wild — as it did in North American and around the world in the late 1970s and early 1980s — gold and silver multiplied in value, while stocks and bonds tumbled. The fact that gold prices move in the same direction as inflation can be an attractive, comforting thought.

Furthermore, political tensions do not affect the value of gold, as they can some other kinds of investment, such as real estate. And its many uses — in coins, medals, jewelry, dentistry, and even electronics — should not be ignored; demand for gold will probably increase, while the amount of gold in the earth will never increase, which will keep its value high.

How To Invest in Precious Metals

There are three essential ways to catch the gold (and silver) bug: purchase it directly; buy stocks in companies that prospect, find, process, and produce gold; or purchase mutual funds that buy gold stocks as part of their portfolios. Let's look at each.

Buying Direct

Purchasing precious metals directly is not unlike purchasing real estate directly, as just noted in MORTGAGES, above. If you buy a house and rent it out, you have to worry about taxes, mortgages, insurance, repairs, tenants, and more. If you buy gold bars through a financial institution, you must store the 1-to-100-ounce wafers and one-kilogram bars somewhere to keep them safe, and make sure you can get to them easily. An easier way to purchase gold directly is by buying bullion coins, such as the Canadian Maple Leaf or the American Eagle. Gold coins are legal tender in many countries, but for tax purposes they are seen as property, much like an automobile or house. This means taking your capital gains (or losses) into account on your income taxes when they are sold. In all provinces except Alberta, there is a sales tax on gold coins. Overall, buying precious metals directly is like buying a fixer-upper house as a real estate investment; it's hardly the easiest way to get a part of the market.

Buying Stock in Gold Companies

This approach is slightly less onerous, and clearly has some advantages. If you check out major gold companies, you may find the prices of some of their stocks attractive. But to quote Pierre Lassonde, "When you buy gold equities you're buying gold that hasn't yet been mined. Making an astute investment will demand an understanding not only of the forces that drive gold prices but also a grasp of the workings of the stock market and the fundamentals of the stock — the company's reserves, production costs, earnings, dividends and management. These fundamentals often require careful homework and a bit of legwork."

In other words, buying stocks of gold producers isn't like buying shares of IBM or Merck. To invest sensibly in precious-metal companies, you *must* be well-informed. You'll need to keep in mind the trading volume of the company, the trend of gold prices, the biases of gold analysts, and much more. It ain't easy. Even a visit to the company's mine in Nevada or South Africa might not be out of order. Bon voyage!

Gold Mutual Funds

Unless you have a lot of time on your hands, and many frequent flier miles for visiting all those distant mines, buying gold mutual funds is an option — but not my recommended opinion. There are certainly no guarantees. Here, as in other sections of this Step, I can suggest ETFs. Here are two: iunits on the TSX, such as Gold Index Fund (XGD), and ishares on AMEX:

Comex Gold Trust (IAU). My personal recommendation — if you are really interested in this type of investment in precious-metals: invest in gold ETFS.

Money Solutions Gold and Other Precious Metals Highlights
 • Gold can be a hedge against runaway inflation, and its use in coins and jewellery will probably increase. But investing in it is still, essentially, a "fool's game."
 • Gold and other precious metals can be purchased directly in wafers and bars from a bank, or as coins. Alternatively, you can purchase the stocks of gold companies, or invest in gold mutual funds. This last approach is by far the easiest.
 • As an investment, gold and other metals leave very much to be desired. Try ETFS, if you insist on this kind of investing.

E. REAL ESTATE

Real estate is usually defined simply as "property, such as land and houses." When most of us think of it, we think of the home we grew up in, or a family cottage, or the house we bought and lived in as a young adult or newlywed. All these residences are indeed real estate, but they only begin to capture its potential. As an investment, real estate can add greatly to — or subtract greatly from, if you're unlucky — a healthy, full investment portfolio.

There are many different kinds of real estate you can invest in: single-family homes, detached houses, condominiums and co-ops, duplexes, three- and four-unit buildings, apartment houses, commercial properties, and mixed-use buildings, which combine residential space with commercial space, such as retail stores on the main floor and apartments above.

Pros and Cons of Investing in Real Estate
The attractions of real estate are many, if only because, like stocks, it tends to be an excellent investment, usually providing returns as high as 8%, 10%, even more. More often than not — although not always — real estate appreciates each year. The profits on a piece of land, a house, or an office building can be astounding, especially over a long period of time. "Buy and Hold" is the recommended strategy for real estate, as it is with quality equity

investments. The fact that you do not pay capital gains tax on the increase in value of your principal residence — the one you live in all year long — means that when you sell it, there could be a real windfall down the road.

Furthermore, real estate can be used as a hedge against inflation, for that inevitable evil can eat away at most other investments far faster than it can the value of land or a building. After all, a company can offer for sale tens of millions of shares of its common stock, but there is inarguably a limited amount of land on this planet. (As the old joke goes, "They're not *making* real estate any more.")

When you invest in real estate directly — i.e., actually buying a property — there are generous possibilities for using leverage, meaning that one can buy land or property with just 10% or even less of the actual price. (See my important **Step 6, below, on Leveraging**). Investing in real estate can also provide wealth for your retirement, if done properly.

The arguments against investing in real estate — especially direct ownership — can be daunting, however. Like any business, real estate is not for the dabbler or the flighty investor. The real estate market goes through cycles, not unlike the stock market, and the prices of land and buildings can fall even more rapidly than they have risen. And under some circumstances, a property can be very, very hard to get rid of. One scholar of real estate noted, "potential investors often believed that real estate was a hands-off, easy way to earn big bucks. People who think this have been watching too many infomercials! Except for a few exceptions, real estate is not an easy business, and it often requires active participation in some form."

In other words, direct investing in real estate is not like purchasing a portfolio of stocks or mutual funds, putting them away in a drawer, and forgetting about them. Nor is buying a piece of real estate like buying a TV set or a car. It might involve everything from costly and time-consuming repairs to collecting rent from delinquent tenants. A lot depends on the method of investment that you choose.

How Do I Invest in Real Estate?
There are primarily three ways: directly, in a limited partnership, or by purchasing mutual funds that invest in real estate properties.

Buying Real Estate Direct

When you purchase land or buildings outright, you have direct control over property that you own. You manage it, subdivide it, search for tenants, etc., and this can have great advantages: you decide everything — the location, the mortgage payments, how much leveraging you will do to raise the money to pay for it, how much to charge your tenants, etc. Naturally, one can hire a property manager to handle many details.

There are important disadvantages to owning real estate directly, however. There is always a liquidity problem — i.e., if you need the money suddenly, you may not be able to sell your land or buildings quickly. You become a landlord, which means you are bound by the Landlord and Tenant Act. You might end up cursed with Tenants From Hell who trash the place or play the drums and have wild parties after midnight. There are taxes to worry about, and city ordinances — all kinds of concerns that you might prefer to avoid, no matter how much you would love to own property directly.

Limited Partnerships

Joining a limited partnership differs from owning real estate directly, in several ways. As a limited partner, your exposure is limited; you have professional management for your land or buildings, so you do not have day-to-day involvement with issues like finding tenants and making sure they pay their rent. Those are nice advantages.

Yet there are disadvantages as well: you still face low liquidity, so it would be difficult to get out of the investment fast. But the largest problem with limited real estate partnerships is probably the number of middlemen involved — each of whom, of course, requires a fee. By the time you are through with packaging a limited partnership, there could be as much as a 50% mark-up on the cost of the properties. Here's an example: *Joe Promoter puts together a limited partnership, then buys several properties. He will typically take up to 10% in fees just to package the deal. Then, there are costs associated with purchasing the properties: real estate fees can be another 6%; then come lawyers' fees and accounting fees. You are already down 30% — and Joe will have to pay out as much as 10% in commissions when he sells the deal.*

Let me attach some numbers to this scenario. Say that you've invested in just one house as a limited partner, and the house cost $200,000. With all the above expenses, its book value — what the partnership paid for it — is $260,000. But its market value is still $200,000; that house has to appreciate in value by 30% just for you to break even! And if real estate prices drop — as they often have, since the late 1980s — you are in even more trouble. If they dip by 30%, the house you invested in would be valued at a mere $140,000. And if you lose a tenant, and can't make your mortgage payment, the bank may foreclose and sell the house; in the current market, it is likely to get $140,000, leaving zero for you. Scenarios like this occur all the time, all around the world. For more on the potentially hellish phenomenon of limited partnerships, **see the first section of this book**, above.

Real Estate Mutual Funds

Equity mutual funds invest in companies; bond mutual funds invest in bonds; it should come as no surprise, therefore, that real estate funds invest in income-producing property, with the goal of achieving long-tem growth through appreciation of the value of the buildings, and the reinvestment of the income. There are very few advantages, if any, to investing in these funds. They are not as liquid as nearly all others; their valuation is usually done only monthly or quarterly, not daily like most mutual funds, so if you want to sell your units, you may have to wait as long as several months. In fact, during rough times in the real estate market, a number of these funds actually suspended redemptions.

Exchange Traded Funds (ETFS)

If you are still determined to invest in real estate in any manner, I once again urge you to consider purchasing real estate ETFs, with which you are purchasing a piece of the entire market, whether it be in Canada, the U.S., Europe, or Asia. Three that come to mind are iunits on the TSX — REIT Index Fund (XRE); and ishares on the AMEX: Cohen & Steers Realty Majors Index Fund (ICF) or Dow Jones U.S. Real Estate Index Fund (IYR).

Money Solutions Real Estate Highlights
   • Investing in real estate is a fascinating, often attractive way of
   investing. There are many strong arguments for investing in real
   estate: it can provide high returns; property nearly always appreciates

in value over the long run; and real estate can be one of the strongest hedges known against the ravages of inflation.

• Arguments against investing in real estate can also be strong, however. Land and houses go through difficult pricing cycles, and managing real estate successfully often demands active participation on the part of the investor.

• You can invest directly, through outright purchase of land or buildings, but that, along with limited partnerships, can require a great deal of time, effort, and luck.

• You can also buy shares in real estate mutual funds, but they are far less liquid than other mutual funds, and they often show poor, even negative returns.

F. STOCKS

The definition of **stocks,** or **equities** (the terms are essentially interchangeable), is hardly frightening in and of itself. Stocks are simply **shares** issued by a company that has "gone public" on a stock exchange. They represent a partial ownership of that business; very partial, of course, as some giant firms of decades standings may have hundreds of millions of shares outstanding, after years of stock-splitting. Imagine the company as a skyscraper, with each brick being a single share of stock. If you own a thousand shares, then 1,000 bricks of that skyscraper belong to you.

Equity simply means ownership. When you have ownership in a business, your equity is your share of that firm, which is represented by a stock certificate. Since you own them, you can do what you like with your shares — keep them or sell them to someone else. Shares are bought and sold at **stock markets;** the price they bring at any given moment is determined quite simply by what other investors are willing to offer for them. Many hundreds of stocks are traded on any given market in the world, and the behaviour of the market in general is measured by an **index** — a representative collection of the stocks on that index. Sometimes their value goes up, and other times down.

It's as simple as that. Yet stocks have long had the reputation of being risky, dangerous things. Think of these classic Milton Berle one-liners for a moment:

"To make a small fortune in stocks, invest a large fortune." "In the old days, stocks split; today, they fall apart." "I call him 'broker' because when I listen to him, that's what I am." "The market today is making a comeback — to 1929."

The last of these gags is the key to the dark humour beneath them all: the stock market crash of 1929, which led to nearly a decade of depression across North America and around the world — and from there, many argue, to runaway inflation, the wiping-out of the life-savings of tens of millions of people like you and me, around the world, the rise of Hitler, fascism, and Communism, and World War II. As I discussed above, in BONDS, to think that history will ever repeat itself in this way is absurd. The Titanic went down, killing some 1500 people, yet the world did not stop taking ocean liners or cruises to the Caribbean. Over a million people on this globe die in automobile accidents every year, yet we don't abandon driving as a mode of transportation.

But the 1929 crash burned its very real pain into the hearts and minds (and investing patterns) of hundreds of millions of people in over a hundred countries, and by doing this, it denied those millions a decent retirement, freedom from worry and poverty, and much more. To this day — nearly eight full decades after that black day on Wall Street — millions still see a common stock as a lottery ticket or casino chip. How sad; how tragic. Because the truth is, equities are *anything* but a silly, chancy bet. They are a first-rate, serious investment — and owning them has huge, proven benefits.

Let us begin our journey through the world of stocks by looking at some of the benefits of owning equity in solid companies.

Benefit #1: Stocks Grow in Value

How likely is it that the stock market will rise at any given time? To listen to the comedians, you would think it was a rare thing. But here are the facts: *the stock market in the United States has gone up approximately three out of four days — 75% of the time — since the mid-1920s.* In fact — and this one may really surprise you — even in a downturn, often called a **bear market**, when the stock market seems to be rolling out of control and down a hill and into an abyss, it closes higher at the end of the day on *four out of ten days.* Not bad odds, surely.

There are many different stock markets around the world, their behaviour measured by various indices. You are probably most familiar with the ones frequently quoted on radio and seen on TV: the Dow Jones Industrial

Average (for the New York Stock Exchange) and the TSX 300 (for the Toronto Stock Exchange). The one most often followed, however, is the Standard & Poor 500, or S&P 500, which is a compilation of the top 500 companies in the United States.

Earlier, I looked at your thoughtful, intelligent grandparents, who invested for you three-quarters of a century ago. But that's a long time, and they invested in the New York Stock Exchange, which may seem a bit scary to many Canadians who read this book. Very well; let me move closer to home and look at how the Toronto Stock Exchange has behaved over the past few decades, and the past few years, in particular. In 1999 alone, the TSX 300 shot up an astonishing 47.4%. (You read right: if you had invested $10,000 in an ETF that followed the TSX, it would have been worth nearly $1,500, twelve months later. Sure beats a GIC or Canada Savings Bond!)

But the record is impressive over most of the years *before* that magical year, and even since. In the three years from 1997 to 1999, the average return was 18.3% a year; over the decade of 1990 through 1999, it averaged a rise of 11.7% annually. To take a longer view, during the 30 years between 1970 and the end of the millennium, the annual average rate of return of the top 300 stocks listed in the TSX index was a strong and healthy 12.6%. (Do note that the last number covers **three traumatic decades** in world history: Trudeau's wage and price controls, the Vietnam War, oil crises, earthquakes, the collapse of the price of gold — along with the Soviet Union, and more. Yet over those tumultuous years, the value of the quality stocks on the TSX 300 index *still* managed to rise over 12% a year! At this rate of return, according to the Rule of 72 (see my comments on that in the first section of this book), the value of one's investment doubles every six years.

The first five years of the 21st century have also been filled with world tumult and chaos: September 11th, 2001, the "crash" of high-tech stocks on NASDAQ, dozens of wars around the world, including in Afghanistan and Iraq. Yet the TSX 300 somehow managed to zoom up 32.27% in 2005, had a 24.32% average over the previous three years, and, since 2001, averaged just under 7% annually. Have there been weak years over those past three decades? Of course; no one ever promised us, or the world markets, a rose garden. But people who have bought — and held — quality equities, or good mutual funds (preferably index or ETFs) over the past three decades, have done very, very well, indeed, since 1970, and the years of Trudeaumania.

Quite simply, major stock **market indices perform better than any other investment** known to man, woman, or child on this earth. They have the potential of being "up" 70 to 75% of the time, and to average over 10% growth each year. (And when we choose to reinvest our dividends, the record is even better.) We would be crazy NOT to invest in the stock market! It is inarguable: stocks grow in value. They do, and they will. Yes, there will always be heart-clutching drops and heart-rejoicing leaps along the way; this behaviour is as much a part of the territory of stock markets as mosquitoes and ants (and yummy picnic lunches) are, when you go camping in the woods. But can the lessons of over three-quarters of a century, and countless research studies since the Great Crash of 1929 be wrong? (That's a rhetorical question; the answer is *no*.)

Benefit #2: Stocks Are a Hedge Against Inflation

If you look back on my entry on INFLATION in the first section of this book, you will see how this insidious force will inevitably cause your hard-earned dollars to lose at least part of their purchasing power. The late 1970s and early 1980s, when inflation hit 20%, were terrifying; comparatively speaking, inflation has been but a minor irritation over the past decade, hovering at less than 2–3% a year. But it can be a killer. Here is what The Great Investor Warren Buffet, has to say on this painful subject: "Recognize the enemy: inflation. The arithmetic makes it plain that inflation is a far more devastating tax than anything that has been enacted by legislature. The inflation tax has a fantastic ability to simply consume capital." True. But by holding quality stocks and passively-invested mutual funds for long periods of time, and reinvesting your dividends by using them to purchase more and more stocks and funds, you can cut back considerably on the cancerous impact of inflation.

Benefit #3: Stocks Can Generate Income

When you receive income from your bank savings accounts, bonds, treasury bills, or mortgages, it is interest income. When you receive income from stocks, it is in the form of **dividends**. As you saw in my entry on dividends in the first section, *you receive far better treatment from Ottawa on your dividend income than you do with interest income.* All smart investors keep this substantial benefit in mind.

Benefit #4: Stocks Offer Important Tax Advantages

The increase in value of your stocks represents capital gains rather than income. Capital gains have three major tax advantages (see my capital gains entry in the first section, above for more detail): Remember, you pay no taxes on capital gains until you sell your investment; the tax on capital gains is lower than taxes on any other income you bring in; and capital gains could pass on to your beneficiaries (your spouse, your children, etc.) tax-free.

Are You Sold Yet?

Now that I have sold you — I hope — on the inevitability of making money by holding good stocks over long periods — yes, *inevitability* — how does one go about investing in them? There are essentially four main ways: by purchasing individual stocks; mutual funds; segregated funds; or Exchange-traded funds (ETFs).

1. Investing in Individual Stocks

Purchasing the stocks of a single company (or of many individual companies) has great potential to generate wealth, but many potential hazards as well. Many people love to point out that $10,000 invested in Coca-Cola's shares in 1980, a quarter century ago, would today — with all the stock splits and dividends reinvested — be worth well over $600,000. The problem is, few other companies can claim such an astounding rate of return, which averaged over 20% a year, on average. But then, plenty of firms *do* show solid returns, year after year.

The catch: many do not. If you, or your parents, had chosen, back in 1980, to put their $10,000 savings into Joe's Cola, or some other brand which sounded good at the time but didn't do well, there might possibly be nothing left at all in your portfolio. Clearly, **when you choose to invest directly in individual stocks, there are many risks involved.** The advantage is clear: you can make a fortune if you choose the "right stock." The disadvantage is, of course, the opposite, and you could lose it all.

Active Trading vs. a Buy-and-Hold Approach

I have discussed, in my entry on Market Timing in the first section of this book, how absurd it is, to leap in and out of the market. Doing so means that you risk missing out on the huge leaps forward that can take place, and have taken place, at countless times — even single days — over the past century. The sensible approach is to buy quality stocks and hold them. This isn't always as easy as it sounds, for two reasons. The first is that it's easy to panic during a downturn. Try your best to keep your emotions out of your investing strategy. It's not easy, but the more you succeed in this, the more money you will end up with, from your investments.

The second factor at work against buy-and-hold investing is that Wall Street and Bay Street do not have the best interests of investors at heart. They never have and they never will. Wall Street and Bay Street want to keep investors in the dark about both the academic evidence on how markets really work, and the dismal track records of the vast majority of active managers. Since the dawn of the retail brokerage business, both brokers and financial planners have had a strong incentive to get customers to trade, and trade often, when it is often in the clients' best interests to do nothing at all — simply to hold on tight to their stocks and mutual funds.

The only winners in the game of active money management are the Wall Street and Bay Street firms that generate commissions, the business publications that offer "expert advice," and our government, which is always collecting more taxes. Legendary investor Peter Lynch offers this advice: "*To the rash and impetuous stock picker who chases hot tips and rushes in and out of equities, an 'investment' in stocks is no more reliable than throwing away paychecks on horses with the prettiest names or the jockey with the purple silks. . . . [But] when you lose [at the racetrack, at least] you'll be able to say you had a great time doing it.*" The lesson should be clear by now: **Don't trade constantly. Buy and hold.** Just make sure that the stocks you purchase give you equity in great companies, whether in Canada, the U.S., or overseas. And there are many hundreds of fine stocks, and companies, to choose from.

From Whom Should You Buy Your Stocks?
There are two ways to do this: through full-service brokers and through discount brokers. The former may be expected to give you considerable advice (not necessarily good advice, of course!), and will charge you a "transaction expense." Discount brokers are the other way to buy and sell equities. These include such well-known names as Ameritrade Canada, Bank of Montreal InvestorLine, E• Trade Canada, Scotia Discount Brokerage, TD Waterhouse,

and several others. You won't get much investment advice, but you can have trades made on your behalf through a web page or over the telephone. The fees are much lower than with a full-service broker, sometimes as low as $40-50 a trade. If you don't need the assistance and "information," you can save some money by purchasing your stocks this way — leaving you more to invest wisely and well.

1. Investing in Equity Mutual Funds Actively Managed Funds

Despite all the wild popularity of mutual funds, the sad reality is, it's next to impossible for the average investor in an actively-managed fund to make the kind of fabulous returns that are published regularly in newspapers and magazines. At the risk of repeating important points (and complaints!) that I've made throughout this book, here are some of the primary reasons why you will *never* get rich from purchasing actively-managed funds:

> • The returns of the vast majority of mutual funds simply fail to keep up with the market indices. In other words, each year, nearly every fund falls below what you would have made had you simply invested directly into those index funds or ETFs, which follow the Dow Jones 30, S&P 500, or the TSX 300.
> • Mutual funds charge you as much as 3% each year in manage your investments, even if they are mainly in cash! (You know — while they wait for the next "best time" to leap back into the mar-ketplace — when nearly *all* the time is the best time!) Does this make any sense to you? Even your bank, which is well known for hitting you for a few bucks, every time you use an ATM or even smile at a teller, doesn't have the gall to charge you such an outra-geous sum for doing absolutely nothing with your money!
> • In addition to the management fee of up to 3% — for rarely, if ever, doing better than a passively invested fund — you could pay a further 5% in commissions to your financial advisor. Do you really need a mutual funds salesperson to charge you 1/20th of your investment, even more (either up front or in a deferred sales charge) *to get you to sell low and buy high*? This is madness! Think about it: most people would be *thrilled* to make 5% on a GIC or Canada Savings Bond, and here you are,

throwing away an unnecessary $5 on every $100 you invest, often for bad advice and very little wisdom!

• Mutual funds can force you to pay taxes (through Capital Gains), through *other investors'* capital gains!

• Most mutual fund managers have a reckless disregard for the dangers — not to mention the sheer stupidity! — of market timing. So, you are risking your hard-earned money (up to 3% management expense ratio) AND a possible additional 5% in commission fees — on an investment strategy that works perhaps once in 10 times, and more often once in 100 — by sheer chance.

2. Investing in Exchange-Traded Funds (ETFS)

Call them **Index Funds**, call them iUnits, call them exchange-traded funds (ETFS), but most important of all — CALL THEM. And BUY them. These are one of the fastest-growing investment vehicles in North America, and with good reason. The attractiveness of ETFS has the potential to make mutual funds obsolete, and to significantly reduce investments in individual stocks, and that's just fine with this writer. (Please remember: between the late 1980s and 1990s, I was the co-founder, President, and Chief Executive Officer of one of the largest financial planning firms in Canada, which made millions and millions of dollars from exactly that: selling mutual funds and stocks. Yet I think back now — like a reformed alcoholic — and my heart sinks when I think of how much better I could have done for my clients, and, yes, for myself, had I been more aware of the then-young concept of ETFS. The mutual fund industry, which grew so fat and complacent over the past decade-plus, has much to lose, if ETFS gain even more in popularity. But *investors will win* — and that is the goal of this book, and of my life, now.

As noted elsewhere in this book, ETFS are, for all practical purposes, much like open-ended, no-load mutual funds. Like mutual funds, they can be created to represent virtually any index or asset class. So, an ETF that "represents" the TSE 60 Index will look just like a TSE 60 Index Fund — the barometer for Canada's largest-capitalization, blue chip companies.

However, ETFS are not actually mutual funds, so they offer far greater tax efficiency, lower annual operating expenses, and more flexible trading

characteristics. Here is a personal, suggested list of ETFS now available —
there are more, all the time, and with good reason — on the TSX, or Toronto
Stock Exchange:

	iunits on the TSX
SYMBOL	
MSCI International Equity Index RRSP Fund	XIN
S&P 500 Index RSP Fund	XSP
S&P/TSX 60 Capped Index Fund	XIC
S&P/TSX 60 Index Fund	XIU
S&P/TSX Capped Energy Energy Index Fund	XEG
S&P/TSX Capped Financial Index Fund	XFN
S&P/TSX Capped Information Techology Index Fund	XIT
S&P/TSX MidCap Index Fund	XMD
S&P/TSX Composite Index Fund	TTF

And here are more ETFS, called ishares, on the AMEX, and their symbols,
based on their market cap, style, sectors, and other aspects:

I. Market Cap

A. Small Cap	B. Mid Cap
Morningstar Mild Core Index Fund (JKJ)	Morningstar Mild Core Index Fund
Russell 2000 Index Fund (IWM)	Russell Midcap Index Fund (IWR)
Russell 2000 Growth Index Fund (IWO)	Russell Midcap Index Fund (IWP)
Russell 2000 Value Index Fund (IWN)	Russell Midcap Value Index Fund (IWS)
Russell Microcap (tm) Index Fund (IWC)	S&P MidCap 400 Growth Index Fund (IJK)
S&P Small Cap 600 Index Fund (IJR)	S&P MidCap 400 Value Index Fund (IJJ)
S&P Small Cap 600 Index Fund (IJT)	
S&P Small Cap 600 Value Index Fund (IJS)	

C. Large Cap

KLD Select Social (SM) Index Fund (KLD)

Morningstar Large Core Index Fund (JKD)

NYSE 100 Index Fund (NY)

Russell 1000 Index Fund (IWB)

Russell 1000 Growth Index Fund (IWD)

S&P 500 Index Fund (IW)

S&P 500 Growth Index Fund (IVW)

S&P 500 Growth Index Fund (IVE)

S&P 100 Index Fund (OEF)

D. Broad U.S. Market

Dow Jones U.S. Total Market Index Fund (IYY)

NYSE Composite Index Fund (NYC)

Russell 3000 Index Fund (IWV)

Russell 3000 Value Index Fund (IWW)

S&P 1500 Index Fund (ISI)

II. Style

A. Value

Morningstar Small Value Index Fund (JKL)

Morningstar Mid Value Index Fund (JKI)

Morningstar Large Value Index Fund (JKF)

Russell Midcap Value Index Fund (IWS)

Russell 3000 Value Index Fund (IWW)

Russell 2000 Value Index Fund (IWN)

Russell 1000 Value Index Fund (IWD)

S&P SmallCap 600 Value Index Fund (IJS)

S&P MidCap 400 Value Index Fund (IJJ)

S&P 500 Value Index Fund (IVE)

B. Growth

Morningstar Small Growth Index Fund (JKK)

Morningstar Mid Growth Index Fund (JKH)

Morningstar Large Growth Index Fund (JKE)

Russell Midcap Growth Index Fund (IWP)

Russell 3000 Growth Index Fund (IWZ)

Russell 2000 Growth Index Fund (IWO)

Russell 1000 Growth Index Fund (IWF)

S&P SmallCap 600 Growth Index Fund (IJT)

S&P MidCap 400 Growth Index Fund (IJK)

S&P 500 Growth Index Fund (IVW)

III. Sector/Industry

A. Basic Materials

Dow Jones U.S. Basic Materials Sector Index Fund (IYM)

B. Consumer Services and Consumer Goods

Dow Jones U.S. Consumer Services Sector Index Fund (IYC)

C. Energy

Dow Jones U.S. Energy Sector Index Fund (IYE)

D. Financial

Cohen & Steers Realty Majors Index Fund (ICF)

Dow Jones U.S. Financial Sector Index Fund (IYF)

Dow Jones U.S. Financial Services Index Fund (IYG)

Dow Jones U.S. Real Estate Index Fund (IYR)

S&P Global Financials Sector Index Fund (IXG)

E. Healthcare

Dow Jones U.S. Healthcare Sector Index Fund (IYH)

Nasdaq Biotechnology Index Fund (IBB)

S&P Global Healthcare Sector Index Fund (IXJ)

F. Natural Resources

Goldman Sachs Natural Resources Index Fund (IGE)

G. Technology

Dow Jones U.S. Technology Sector Index Fund (IYW)

Goldman Sachs Networking Index Fund (IGN)

Goldman Sachs Semiconductor Index Fund (IGW)

Goldman Sachs Software Index Fund (IGV)

Goldman Sachs Technology Index Fund (IGM)

S&P Global Technology Sector Index Fund (IXN)

H. Telecommunications

Dow Jones U.S. Telecommunications Sector Index Fund (IYZ)

S&P Global Telecommunications Sector Index Fund (IXP)

I. Utilities

Dow Jones U.S. Utilities Sector Index Fund (IDU)

IV. International

A. Europe

MSCI Austria Index Fund (EWO)

MSCI Belgium Index Fund (EWK)

MSCI EMU Index Fund (EZU)

MSCI France Index Fund (EWQ)

MSCI Germany Index Fund (EWG)

MSCI Italy Index Fund (EWI)

MSCI Netherlands Index Fund (EWN)

MSCI Spain Index Fund (EWP)

MSCI Sweden Index Fund (EWD)

MSCI Switzerland Index Fund (EWL)

MSCI United Kingdom Index Fund (EWU)

S&P Europe 350 Index Fund (IEV)

B. Asia

FTSE/Xinhua China 25 Index Fund (FXI)

MSCI Australia Index Fund (EWA)

MSCI Hong Kong Index Fund (EWH)

MSCI Japan Index Fund (EWJ)

MSCI Malaysia Index Fund (EWM)

MSCI Pacific ex-Japan Index Fund (EPP)

MSCI Singapore Index Fund (EWS)

MSCI South Korea Index Fund (EWY)

MSCI Taiwan Index Fund (EWT)

S&P/TOPIX 150 Index Fund (ITF)

C. Africa

MSCI South Africa Index Fund (EZA)

D. Americas

MSCI Brazil Index Fund (EWZ)

MSCI Canada Index Fund (EWC)

MSCI Mexico Index Fund (EWW)

S&P Latin America 40 Index Fund (ILF)

E. Global

MSCI EAFE Index Fund (EFA)

MSCI EAFE Value Index Fund (EFV)

MSCI EAFE Growth Index Fund (EFG)

S&P Global Energy Sector Index Fund (IXC)

S&P Global Financials Sector Index Fund (IXG)

S&P Global Healthcare Sector Index Funds (IXJ)

S&P Global Technology Sector Index Fund (IXN)

S&P Telecommunications Sector Index Fund (IXP)

S&P Global 100 Index Fund (IOO)

F. Regional

MSCI EMU Index Fund (EZU)

MSCI Pacific ex-Japan Index Fund (EPP)

S&P Europe 350 Index Fund (IEV)

S&P/TOPIX 150 Index Fund (ITF)

S&P Latin America 40 Index Fund (ILF)

G. Emerging Markets

FTSE/Xinhua China 25 Index Fund (FXI)

MSCI Emerging Markets Index Fund (EEM)

MSCI Brazil Index Fund (EWZ)

MSCI Malaysia Index Fund (EWM)

MSCI Mexico Index Fund (EWW)

MSCI South Africa Index Fund (EZA)

MSCI South Korea Index Fund (EWY)

MSCI Taiwan Index Fund (EWT)

S&P Latin America 40 Index Fund (ILF)

V. Specialty/Real Estate

A. Real Estate

Cohen & Steers Realty Majors Index Fund (ICF)

Dow Jones U.S. Real Estate Index Fund (IYR)

B. Specialty

Dow Jones Select Dividend Index Fund (DVY)

Dow Jones Transportation Average Index Fund (IYT)

Dow Jones U.S. Financial Services Index Fund (IYG)

Goldman Sachs Technology Index Fund (IGM)

Goldman Sachs Natural Resources Index Fund (IGE)

Goldman Sachs Networking Index Fund (IGN)

Goldman Sachs Semiconductor Index Fund (IGW)

Goldman Sachs Software Index Fund (IGV)

KLD Select Social (SM) Index Fund (KLD)

Nasdaq Biotechnology Index Fund (IBB)

As you can see, ETFS are hardly a Baskin-Robbins choice, or even a *101 Dalmatians* choice. You can truly simplify your investment portfolio — and do much better than you've ever done in the past — with thoughtful consideration and selection of the many ETFS listed above.

Let me share some further thoughts about a few examples of ETFS which I have personally followed over the past few years, only some of which I have shared earlier. *ETFS in Canada shot up 28% in 2005, and a total of 34% over three years. Brazil's ETFS zoomed 52% in 2005; 63% over three years; and — if you purchased ETFS "playing" the Index of the U.S. "Energy Sector," to give you merely one example, that one increased in value by 34% in 2005. And the ETFS covering the "Financial Sector" of Canada moved up 23% in 2005.*

Pretty amazing. But here is something to make your stomach churn, if you haven't considered ETFS before reading about them here: ***three of the largest "actively managed" mutual fund companies in Canada*** (AIC, CI and TD) averaged a respective increase of 14%, 22% and 20% in 2005, but **averaged only 12%, 19% and 9% annually over the past three years**. And the same three mutual fund companies, when dealing with **U.S. stocks**, went up only 9%, .5% and 3% respectively in 2005, and *averaged only 2%, 6% and 1%, over the past three years!* Compare *those* gains with ETFS which invested, in 2005, in Mexico (up 46%), South Korea (55%), Japan (25%), and the Emerging Markets sector (34%), and you can see what you may have been missing.

Putting one's money inside your mattress has never seemed more enticing! Although it seems pretty clear that the "simple" way — to invest in indices, with ETFS (which carry very, very low charges for "service"), obviously does better — wildly better — than with those so-called "bright market-timers" who earn whopping salaries at the mutual funds companies.

Here are some additional reasons why ETFS are such an attractive investment:

1. They are far more precise as tools in portfolio building.
2. They outperform most mutual funds, most of the time.
3. They are far more consistent and less risky than individual stocks.
4. The trading price of an ETF is approximately equal to the

trading value of the underlying securities held in the fund, plus any distributed income.

5. There are no redemption fees when units are sold on the exchange; only customary brokerage commissions need apply.
6. You can trade an entire portfolio of stocks in a single transaction.
7. You can easily get complete information about the index which underlies your particular ETF. This means transparent, easy-to-track investments.
8. You get continuous real-time quotations easily, and can trade any time during regular office hours.
9. There are no minimum purchases. IUnits are usually bought and sold in the exact same way as stocks.
10. Investments in ETFS avoid the Loser's Game of stock picking and market timing.

In conclusion, I hope I've made it very clear: stocks can, and do, grow in value, often greatly. Is there risk in investing in the stock markets of the world? I would strongly suggest to you — after over a quarter-century in this industry — that the *real* risk in investing is NOT to be invested in the stock markets of the world — especially in equities themselves, or, better yet, equity index instruments such as index funds and ETFS.

Money Solutions Stocks Highlights
• **In spite of normal, daily fluctuation of markets, equities represent a serious investment, and no gamble.**
• **Stocks can-and do-grow in value, often greatly. Since the mid-1920s, the prices of stocks have gone up 75% of the time. The real risk in investing is NOT to be invested in the stock markets of the world-especially in equities themselves, or equity index instruments such as index funds and ETFS.**
• **Stocks are a superb hedge against inflation, and can generate income through their dividends-income that has major tax advantages.**
• **The arguments for purchasing passive index funds, as opposed to actively managed funds, are persuasive.**

• It is wise to diversify your holdings by investing in several stock-market indexes, in different parts of the world, and/or focusing on different industries, such as health, technology, energy, etc.
• You can also invest in index stocks, or ETFs-an innovative product for the knowledgeable and intelligent investor that combines the advantages of index investing and holding shares of stock. Don't forget: active managers underperform their benchmarks not only in bull markets, but also in bear markets!

G. TREASURY BILLS

Treasury Bills, or T-bills, are short-term investments that often last as little as 91, 182, or 364 days. They are issued by the Government of Canada every Friday and bought at a discount to their face value. Thus, you purchase these "obligations of the government" at less than their par value, and they mature at par. The difference between the issue price and the par value of the T-bill reaches at maturity is your return on the short-term loan you have made to the federal government. T-bills do not appear to pay interest, but that eventual gain is taxed as interest income to the purchaser.

Since the usual face value of a T-bill is $10,000, $100,000, or more, until recently it was only the occasional wealthy individual investor who would join the banks, trust companies, and corporations in purchasing them. More recently, many of these institutions began to offer "pieces" of these large treasury bills in denominations as low as $1,000, which attracted to them a growing number of investors more like the average Canadian.

Advantages of T-bills
The most obvious reason to want to purchase a treasury bill is the impressive credentials of the "company" offering them for sale every week: the Govern-ment of Canada. T-bills are guaranteed by this well-known borrower in the same way as Canada Savings Bonds and guaranteed investment certificates (GICs). The knowledge that these bills are insured (up to $60,000 worth) has allowed many a fearful investor to sleep better at night.

There are other reasons many people find T-bills attractive. Their yield — in other words, their rate of return — has often exceeded that of Canada

Savings Bonds, and is *always* greater than the insulting amount paid by your local bank on your so-called Premium Savings Account. Compared with other major "guaranteed" ways of investing, T-bills come out on top, in terms of money earned.

Disadvantages of T-bills

Quite simply, T-bills do NOT offer very large returns. When you purchase them, you are lending our federal government money for a very brief period of time. I've discussed elsewhere in these pages that it is far, far better to be an "owner," purchasing equity in a company through its common stocks, than a "loaner," handling money over to a company or government for a while, which gives you no real "piece of the action." Owners beat out loaners, in potential financial gain, 99 times out of 100.

Furthermore, the return you get from T-bills is as heavily taxed as the interest received on a savings bond, which slashes away at almost any possible profit, especially when inflation is factored in. I personally like to say that "the 'T' in T-bills could well stand for 'timid' and 'tiny returns.'"

How To Invest in T-bills

T-bills, like most bonds, are traded in multiples of $1,000. They are generally traded by brokers, banks, major businesses, and a few large investors who find themselves with large sums that they want to lend for very short periods of time. The bills are often subject to minimum purchases of $5,000 to $10,000. However, individual investors who find T-bills attractive can purchase them in smaller amounts, by investing in Canadian Treasury Bill money market funds. Many large mutual fund companies offer these funds, which have extremely low management expense ratios (MERs) — usually around ½%, far less than you would pay for most other mutual funds. (But not better, interestingly, than the MER for most ETFs.)

But *what are you getting?* Andex Associates of Windsor, Ontario, one of the most respected researchers of investment returns, once showed that over the 30-year period between 1970 and 2000, U.S. stocks averaged an annual return of 15%, Canadian stocks, 12.6%, guaranteed investment certificates 9.5%, and treasury bills only 8.5%. Yes, that's better than your savings account at the bank, but *T-bills are clearly not the most effective way to make your money grow*. Far from it.

Money Solutions Treasury Bills Highlights
• Treasury bills have advantages, it's true: they are government-backed, with CDIC insurance behind them. And their yield is often better than the return from savings bonds, and always much better than bank savings accounts.
• The returns are not huge from T-bills. They are a loan to the government, and not a purchase of a piece of a company, like a stock. They are highly taxed, as well.
• Those who fear risk should consider T-bills, but never invest more than 10 or 15% of your portfolio in them; that pleasant 100% guarantee by the government does not make up for the low return, especially after taxes.

H. CREATING AN IDEAL INVESTMENT PORTFOLIO

Now that you have a grasp on the concepts behind successful investment planning, I here offer you my suggestions for creating a winning investment portfolio. (I did not choose to call this book *Retire Early and Wealthy* for *no reason*, I assure you). But no "secrets" or "magic formulas" will be revealed in the next few pages. Investing is about risk and reward, and choosing the strategy that is most likely to deliver the expected results over time. I do not profess to have knowledge to predict certain outcomes, nor does anyone else. But, my many years of hands-on experience, and some costly mistakes, have taught me that — since no one can predict the outcome — *it is prudent to plan in such a way that you minimize the chance of losing, and maximize the chance of winning.*

If you are planning to take a trip to a place where you've never visited before, it's helpful to check out a road map and prepare a plan. An investment road map or plan is called an **Investment Policy Statement**, or IPS. Pensions funds, which often handle many billions of dollars, would *never* invest before first determining an IPS. *Your* IPS should address three very important issues:

1. How long is your investment horizon?
2. What are your financial objectives?

3. What is your tolerance for risk?

Let us first take a look at the **investment horizon**. The length of time you have to invest is important, because of the risks that are inherent in equity investing. *The longer the investment horizon, the greater the chances that you will achieve the expected results from equity investments.* The table below suggests a reasonable guideline for allocating your funds between equity and fixed income:

INVESTMENT HORIZON (YEARS)	EQUITY ALLOCATION (%)	FIXED-INCOME ALLOCATION (%)
Less than 3	0	100
4	10	90
5	20	80
6	30	70
7	40	60
8	50	50
9	60	40
10	70	30
11–15	80	20
16+	90	10

Knowing your **financial objectives** is also important when creating an ideal investment portfolio. For example, let's say you are investing to make sure you have enough funds for your retirement years. Most people underestimate their life expectancy greatly, and as a result, do *not* plan their investment strategies prudently. According to the National Center for Health Statistics in the United States (and I sense that the numbers may not be much different in Canada), the following statistics should be used when planning for your retirement years:

ADDITIONAL YEARS YOU SHOULD PLAN TO LIVE		
AT AGE	MALE	FEMALE
55	32	36
60	27	31
65	22	27
70	18	22

The above numbers are rising all the time, of course, with improved health care, more people exercising, many eating more healthily, and so on.

Last, but not least, it is important that you understand your **tolerance for risk**. Consider this scenario: your investment horizon is 20 years and your objective is to have enough money to generate sufficient income for your retirement. You then determine that your expected rate of return must be 12% compounded over those 20 years. You conclude that to achieve this return, you would have to invest 90% of your funds in equities. However, you are the type of person who stays awake at night worrying, and you are a nervous wreck when it comes to "taking risks." So *what do you do?* Here are a couple of options:

> • You could reduce your expected rate of return, which means you will have to reduce your expectations of your retirement income.
> • You could change your attitude about risk and accept the fact that risk is significantly reduced as your time horizon increases. Twenty years is *sufficient* time for you to weather the ups and downs of the market and come out a winner.

Constructing the Portfolio
Portfolio construction is not a science. There is no "right" portfolio. However, there are a few good rules to follow:

> • Regardless of the asset class, use only index or passive asset class funds. Active management, as I've pointed out so many times above, is a loser's game.
> • Diversify across many asset classes. Virtually all of the returns — as much as 94%! — from a portfolio are determined by asset allocation decisions. Stock selection and market timing account for less than 3%.
> • Generally avoid long-term bonds, and *always* avoid bond funds. For the fixed-income portion of a portfolio, use only short-term fixed income instruments.

A Sample Portfolio

The following assumptions are made for this sample portfolio: the time horizon is 15 years; and the amount of the investment is $100,000 (but the same strategy could be applied to investing $10,000 or $10-million).

RECOMMENDED ASSET ALLOCATION FOR
A $100,000 INVESTMENT PORTFOLIO

TYPE OF INVESTMENT	PORTION OF TOTAL	AMOUNT
Equities	80%	$80,000
Fixed Income	20%	$20,000

Your next step will be to determine what your specific investments should be in each category listed above.

Equities (80% or $80,000)

I have demonstrated how a passive investment strategy is the only kind you should embrace, if you want to invest like the winners. Exchange-Traded Funds (ETFS) offer effective asset allocation and diversification.

A SAMPLE ETF EQUITY PORTFOLIO

INDUSTRY	SYMBOL	% OF INVESTMENT	AMOUNT
TSE	TTF	25%	$20,000
DJIA	DIA	25%	$20,000
S&P 500	SPY	25%	$20,000
Nasdaq	QQQ	25%	$20,000

For further diversification, if the amount of your investment is larger, you could consider ETFS in various *sectors*. In Canada, for example, you could invest in the following sectors:

ETFS SYMBOL	PORTFOLIO
TSX 60 Capped Index Fund	Large-cap Canadian Equity XIC
TSX Canadian Mid-Cap Fund	Mid-cap Canadian Equity XMD
TSX Canadian Financials Fund	Canadian Financials Sector XFN
TSX Canadian Technology Fund	Canadian IT Sector XIT
TSX Canadian Energy Fund	Canadian Energy Sector XEG

Many more sub-indices, or sector ETFs, are available in the U.S. markets, as you have seen in the previous section on Stocks.

Fixed Income (20% or $20,000)

The only investment you should consider for *the fixed-income portion* of your portfolio is five-year Government of Canada bonds.

Rebalancing Your Portfolio

Even when your funds are allocated into different asset classes, no outcome can be guaranteed. However, to maximize your chances of success, it is very important that your portfolio not drift too far away from your Investment Policy Statement (IPS). Without **rebalancing**, market movements will cause your portfolio to depart from your desired percentage mix.

A simple example will illustrate this point. Let's revisit the earlier sample portfolio and summarize your initial asset mix:

INVESTMENT	% OF TOTAL	VALUE OF INVESTMENT
Equities (80% or $80,000)		
TSX (TTF)	20%	$20,000
DJIA (DIA)	20%	$20,000
S&P 500 (SPY)	20%	$20,000
Nasdaq (QQQ)	20%	$20,000
Fixed Income (20% or $20,000)		
Canadian Bond Broad Market (XBB)	10%	$10,000
Government of Canada 5-yr.		
Bond Fund (XGV)	10%	$10,000

Now suppose that, one year later, you have experienced the following outcomes in the performance of your investments:

INVESTMENT	RATE OF RETURN	VALUE OF INVESTMENT	% OF TOTAL
Equities			
TSX (TTF)	+12%	$22,400	21.0%
DJIA (DIA)	+15%	$23,000	21.5%
S&P 500 (SPY)	+20%	$24,000	22.5%
Nasdaq (QQQ)	-18%	$16,400	15.3%
Subtotal		$85,800	80.3%

INVESTMENT	RATE OF RETURN	VALUE OF INVESTMENT	% OF TOTAL
Fixed Income			
Bonds	+5%	$21,000	19.7%
Subtotal		$21,000	19.7%
Total		$106,800	100.0%

To maintain your desired asset allocation mix, your portfolio will have to be rebalanced as follows:

	NEW ASSET ALLOCATION	
INVESTMENT	% OF TOTAL	VALUE OF INVESTMENT
Equities (80%)		
TSX (TTF)	20%	$21,360
DJIA (DIA)	20%	$21,360
S&P 500 (SPY)	20%	$21,360
Nasdaq (QQQ)	20%	$21,360
Fixed Income (20%)		
Bonds	20%	$21,360
Total	100%	$106,800

To achieve these desired results, you will have to take the following steps:

1. "Sell" shares with the following dollar values:
   — TSX (TFF): $1,040
   — DJIA (DIA): $1,640
   — S&P 500 (SPY): $2,640
2. "Buy" shares with the following dollar values:
   — NASDAQ (QQQ): $4,960
   — Bonds: $360

Not only will this rebalancing of your asset mix meet your desired investment objective as per your IPS, but you will be practicing a winning investment strategy of *buying low* and *selling high*. (The mutual fund and the brokerage industry, unfortunately, practices the **opposite** strategy of *buying* **high** and *selling* **low**.)

Rebalancing allows you to avoid drifting away from your desired asset mix. It should be incorporated into your IPS and done regularly at predetermined intervals or if there are unusual market fluctuations.

What If You Don't Have a "Lump Sum" To Invest?
I've show you how to invest a lump sum of money. But what if you are faced with the following situations?

1. You would like to start an RESP.

2. You have only a small amount to invest in an RRSP.

3. You would like to start a dollar-cost-averaging plan.

4. You want to keep things really simple and use a winning money accumulation strategy.

The solution in the above cases is for you to consider index mutual funds or ETFS.

RECOMMENDED MUTUAL FUNDS

FUND	INSTITUTION
Index Funds	
TD DJIA Index Fund	TD Bank
Royal U.S. Index Fund	Royal Bank
CIBC Canadian Index	CIBC
CIBC U.S. Equity Index	CIBC
CIBC International Index	CIBC
CIBC U.S. Index RRSP	CIBC
CIBC Nasdaq Index RRSP	CIBC

How Do You Take an Income from Your Accumulated Pool of Capital?
You have now achieved your investment objectives and would like an income for your retirement, or to send your child to university. (Congratulations). The most effective way to withdraw funds from your pool of capital is to set up a **Systematic Withdrawal Plan** (SWP). This strategy is so crucial to one's goal of *Retiring Early and Wealthy*, that I have given it a step all its own: **See Step 7, below.**

What, then, have you learned in this very lengthy chapter? That there is no "right" portfolio, and you should choose a diversified portfolio of asset classes. That you should use only passive investments for your portfolio, preferably ETFs. And that you can very well achieve a much more early retirement — and a much more financially lucrative one — than you ever imagined.

Money Solutions Ideal Portfolio Highlights
   • There is no one "right" portfolio, but you can reduce risk by choosing a diversified portfolio of asset classes.
   • Use only passive investments for your portfolio, since active management is nearly always a loser's game.
   • If you do use actively managed mutual funds, the only ones you should consider are those with a "buy-and-hold" philosophy.
   • Keep it simple, and win!

Author's Note:

The next four Steps — on Managing Debt (**Step 4**), Understanding Compound Growth (**Step 5**), the Power of Leveraging (**Step 6**) and Systematic Withdrawal Plans, or swps (**Step 7**) are quite brief, compared with the first three Steps, above. But *in no way should this suggest to the Reader that these are any less important*! I have often made a point in these pages of insisting on **simplicity** in financial matters, and the same can go for **brevity**: It is precisely through an understanding of, and the use of, **Steps 4 through 7**, that investors can *best Retire Early and Wealthy*, as the title of this book urges. Tools such as Leveraging and the swp, for example, can free up large sums of money and make them last much longer. I urge everyone to *consider these last four Steps as seriously as the first three*; they are four more essential keys to success in financial planning.)

STEP 4

LEARN HOW TO
MANAGE YOUR DEBT!

D ebt is the subject of many jokes — "Until debt do us part," etc. — but it's the cause of many suicides as well. But being in debt is not necessarily an evil thing, in spite of what many religious leaders have warned over the centuries. Indeed, there can be such a thing as **"good" or "creative" debt**, such as borrowing money against your home, and then investing it wisely and thoughtfully (see **Step 3**, and all my talk about ETFs being far better than "actively-managed" mutual funds, above), while "writing off" the *interest* on the borrowed sum on your income taxes.

Still, falling into debt is no laughing matter for most. Many people end up trapped in a cycle of "bad" debt, borrowing money all the time to purchase things that will only drop in value, or depreciate, such as an automobile or a plasma TV. I am personally alarmed by the gigantic debts being run up by university students, often thanks to credit card companies handing out credit cards like candy — or like cocaine, which is probably a better simile — on college campuses. (A 2003 study by the U.S. Senate, of all people, found that new university students are bombarded with an average of eight (!) credit cards, *during their first week of school alone.* Canadian numbers must be similar.)

Let's face it, most kids who go away to schools at the age of 18 or 19 have had their parents doing their laundry and buying and paying for their groceries — not to mention making their beds — over the previous two decades; they have **no** idea how to budget, and often find themselves in a No Man's Land of bills and, quickly, large debts. Most of these young people should never use credit cards in the first place. And once they do, they quickly find themselves straddled with 12%, 18%, even 26% annual fees on their monthly bills — costing them hundreds, and even thousands of dollars of wasted money, that they *should* be investing in ETFs. I recently read that North America now has the highest percentage of "bankrupt kids" in the history of universities, and this sickens me. Then, they must rush off into the workforce (without traveling or enjoying themselves first), since they have all these bills to pay off. (And I haven't even mentioned the tens of thousands, sometimes even $100,000+, which American students find themselves owing after four years of high college tuitions, room, board, books, loans, and so on.)

This is a pattern among young people in Canada as well. To quote a recent *Maclean's* story from early 2006 (which is sub-titled "Meet the Debt Generation"), "While all Canadians are feeling the pinch of rising debt levels, young people are being squeezed the hardest." This was clearly — and rather depressingly — proven in a recent report by the Vanier Institute for the Family: *the average net worth (which is one's assets, less their debt) for Canadian youth under the age of 25 dropped by a shocking 95% between 1984 and 1999!* The fact that approximately one-half of all unmarried women and men between the ages of 20 and 34 are still living with their parents is one thing; the fact that most are drowning in debt, and have pretty well zero savings — so they are certainly not putting much money into RRSPS or investing in stock markets, and taking advantage of compound growth (see **Step 5, below**).

I could go on and on — including the fact that these same young people — and many of their parents, sadly — soon find themselves needing to go into "good debt" — such as the financing of a much-needed car, or a condo or house — but they find themselves lacking the good credit rating they must have, in order to obtain that car or house loan! One possibility is a **PrePaid Credit Card**, also known as **Secure Credit Cards**, which are available from Visa, MasterCard, and other giant companies. I was intrigued by the offering of a company called *mint*, which offers prepaid MasterCard cards. Let me quote from their website: "Consumers can achieve financial freedom by carrying a prepaid card to which they can transfer weekly or monthly spending budgets, and use where and when required. Record keeping is made simpler through online presentment of statements and transaction records. The temptation to dip into lines of credit or savings accounts is removed."

But how can they even make that payment up-front, if they are already sinking into debts, and paying usurious interest fees on their too-many-credit-cards? And we talk endlessly and fearfully about *drug* addictions? When we see that the average Canadian household is carrying close to $10,000 in credit card debt — up from "only" $3,000, just 15 years ago, forcing the average family to spend close to $1.25 for every dollar they earn, we have some major debt problems in our country.

There are warning signs, of which we should all be aware:

• Do you find that you are constantly concerned about your monetary situation?
• Are you always paying your bills late?
• Have you started to get frequent calls from individual creditors, even collection agencies, about "unpaid bills"?
• Have you "maxed-out" your credit cards, and begun to carry large amounts forward each month, paying only "the minimum amount due"?
• Is a larger and larger amount of your net income going to cover merely the interest on the debts you owe, without even touching the ever-growing principal?

There are many ways — none of them guaranteed — to crawl out of The Debt Pit; here are a few suggestions:

a. Like a smoker trying to quit, **make an outright promise to yourself that you will start paying cash for everything you buy, from today on. Vow to commit up to one-fourth of your net income to paying off those ever-rising debts.**

b. **Look around for cheaper credit.** Gas stations and retail stores often charge up to 28% in interest, even more, and the average of most bank credit cards (Visa, MasterCard, etc.), may be as high as 18%, even more. But there are other cards available which charge a *fraction* of that rate, even if only for the first year. (I've seen some that offer 1.5% a month for the first six months, if you transfer over your debt). *A few minutes of research, over the phone or on the Internet, can save you thousands!*

c. **Consider refinancing everything you now owe to all of those creditors.** If you own a home, and can take out a second mortgage at, say, 10% interest, or a line of credit or home equity loan at prime, this surely beats that 19% or 26% credit card debt which has been slowly bleeding you to death! *Consolidate all of your debts, if possible, into one monthly payment, and then pay it — somehow.*

d. We all have priorities in life, yes? Our kids first, spouse second, parents third (perhaps). . . . If suggestion "c" isn't feasible, then **try the Priority Route with your debts:** *pay off the most expensive, highest-interest debts* (to that clothing store; to that gas station) FIRST, *and then chip away at the others, which cost you less.*

e. If you find that you cannot live without a credit card, then at the very least, **make sure that you repay the entire amount owing, IN FULL, every single month.** And check out how each, individual card works, because some allow you up to 50 days of interest-free credit each month; in other words, many allow you to purchase things on the very first day of the monthly credit cycle, and then pay the full amount due on the last day. It's legal, Visa, MC and AmEx will hate you for doing this, but that's fine; those companies are worth billions, and you're struggling to get debt-free.

f. **Let your creditors know that you are struggling.** Some may allow you to stretch out your payments, if you can possibly repay them on a regular basis, and now and then, they may even waive late penalties. It's certainly worth a try.

g. Maybe toughest of all: **learn to discipline yourself.** (Shades of quitting the weed or losing that weight, but it's essential). *Use cash as often as you can; stick to a budget; make sure you start saving every month; invest when you can (ever heard of ETFs?), as soon as your debts are down and manageable.*

You got *into* these debts, remember, and with wise money management, you can get *out* of them, without declaring bankruptcy or selling your home. Remember, the thousands that you may be spending (read "wasting") to pay down your debts, could be growing by leaps and bounds in wise (and simple!) investments. So, you're not **merely** paying thousands in usury-like payments of up to 30% annual charges; you are LOSING those thousands, times 10–20% every year in possible gains, in good investments. Good luck.

Money Solutions on Managing Your Debt Highlights
   • Most Canadians do not know how to budget, and the percentage of those in serious debt is growing enormously.
   • There are warning signs, ranging from paying your bills late, to maxed-out credit cards, to wasting money on interest payments on debts you owe.
   • There are several ways to crawl out of the Debt Pit: pay cash, find cheaper credit rates, refinance, learn to discipline yourself, and more.

STEP 5

UNDERSTAND COMPOUND GROWTH

I love the answer that one of the greatest minds of the past several centuries once gave. The man was Albert Einstein; the question was *"What is the most powerful thing on earth?"* His (purported) reply? *"Compound interest."*

It's true. **Compound interest**, *or* **compound growth**, has the power to make poor people rich, to prevent millions of living or ending their lives in abject poverty, to create great, billion-dollar companies out of tiny start-ups in a garage. The magic number is "The Rule of 72," and it helps you to understand the astonishing **POWER** of Compound Growth. Don't let the number faze you; it's really easy to understand: The Rule of 72, as I noted back in the first section of this book, allows you to determine how long it takes for you to "double your money." It is worth repeating here:

One merely divides the "magic" number of 72 by the expected rate of return on your investment, and what you get is, the number of years that it will take for you to double your money. A good example: let's say you can get a 12% annual return on the money you have invested (in an ETF, I hope). Simply take 72 and divide it by that number — in this case, 12 — and you get the number 6. So, at 12%, it will take six years to double that money. Not bad! Study these two very straight-forward (and, yes, simple!) charts below, and realize both the genius behind "The Rule of 72"), as well as the stunning glory of Compound Interest. Albert Einstein was right, as you will shortly see:

YEARS	CHART A: Invest $100 per month. . . . ANNUAL RATE OF RETURN				
	5%	8%	10%	12%	15%
5	$6,800	$7,348	$7,744	$8,167	$8,857
10	$15,528	$18,295	$20,484	$23,004	$27,522
15	$26,728	$34,604	$41,447	$49,958	$66,851
20	$41,103	$58,902	$75,937	$98,926	$149,724
25	$59,550	$95,103	$132,683	$187,885	$324,353
30	$83,226	$149,036	$226,049	$349,496	$692,328
35	$113,609	$229,388	$379,664	$643,096	$1,467,718
40	$152,604	$349,101	$632,408	$1,176,477	$3,101,605

As you can see, Compound Growth truly is more powerful than any bomb, atomic, hydrogen or otherwise, which may have originated with Albert Einstein's theory about the power that lies inside mass (in his inspired equation, Energy equals Mass times the speed of light squared). But here is a chart that I love, *almost* as much as the ones above, because it shows that *the "tiny" investment of $ each month that we just observed ends up having far greater value — eventually — than a starting that investment with a "lump sum" of $10,000* — which most of us *don't* have, when we are young. Note how the numbers of the above, which show "regular" and "small" little investments, end up being worth far more, once we pass a certain period of time!

YEARS	CHART B: Invest a Lump Sum of $10,000 ANNUAL RATE OF RETURN				
	5%	8%	10%	12%	15%
5	$12,762	$14,694	$16,105	$17,623	$20,114
10	$16,289	$21,589	$25,937	$31,058	$40,455
15	$20,789	$31,722	$41,722	$54,736	$81,371
20	$26,533	$46,610	$67,275	$96,463	$163,665
25	$33,864	$68,485	$108,347	$170,000	$329,190
30	$43,219	$100,627	$174,494	$299,599	$662,118
35	$55,160	$147,853	$281,024	$527,996	$1,331,755
40	$70,400	$217,245	$452,592	$930,510	$2,678,635

You can discover some amazing things here. One, obviously, is the awesome power of Compound Growth. But another is, of course, the *amazing* difference — over the years — between the eventual amount, if you **invest** wisely and thoughtfully — and, dare I say it again — simply. Just think of *a one-time $10,000 investment in a GIC at 5% over 40 years, going up 7 times!* Not bad. But *if you had chosen to invest, instead, that one-time lump sum into a quality ETF which averaged 15% a year, the eventual total at the end of the same four decades would be over 26 TIMES higher!* (And, need I add, if you lacked that "huge" sum of $10,000, four decades ago, and merely invested that modest $100 a month over the same 40 years, your eventual sum would be *31 times higher*.)

That is the power of Compound Growth, and the importance of regular investing, no matter how small the sum. Providing, of course, that you pay off the debts you have (which are bleeding countless dollars from your possible savings, and thus, many multiples of those dollars, had they been invested in decent-interest-paying financial vehicles!)

Money Solutions Compound Growth Highlights
   • **Compound Growth (or Interest) is one of the most powerful aspects behind successful wealth management.**
   • **It is crucial to maximize your rate of return on an investment by**

even the slightest amount-such as 11% a year rather than 10% — to achieve the greatest results.

• Time is a vital part of the magic of Compound Growth. The longer you leave money in an investment, the more you can expect that amount to grow-often to stunning amounts.

STEP 6

USE THE POWER
OF LEVERAGING
TO CREATE
LONG-TERM WEALTH

The word "leveraging" has the word "lever" in it, and with good reason. Recall the famous saying of an ancient Greek scientist, "if you give me a lever large enough, I could lift the world." (Anyone who has ever used a wheelbarrow, allowing them to lever and move a vastly heavier amount of dirt or cement than they could ever *carry* by themselves, will know even more quickly what I'm talking about.)

The same goes for LEVERAGING. It is simply *the strategy of prudently borrowing money to invest* (one hopes, thoughtfully and creatively). This strategy can allow investors to achieve higher effective rates of return, and accelerate the wealth-building process when utilized over the long term. A person who uses the leveraging strategy to accumulate wealth is much like a long-distance runner who achieves a boost of energy at just the right time.

Leveraging can help every person to achieve their financial goals sooner. *It is not for everyone, however.* The best example of leveraging is the purchase of a home, which the vast majority of people do, through the use of "taking out a mortgage" with a bank or trust company. By putting down a portion of the total amount for the house or condo ("the down payment"), and borrowing the balance ("the mortgage"), the purchaser is using the leveraging strategy to purchase his/her home. Leveraging is:

> *using borrowed funds to maximize the rate of return on investment,"* to quote one financial planner. *But then, he warns, "Keep in mind that losses can amount very quickly if your investment starts losing money." The term is used a lot in real estate: A small fraction down, and by borrowing the rest from a bank, you've leveraged to your advantage.*

Naturally, when the value of your home goes up, you make good money on your investment; leveraging becomes one of the best things you ever did. (**You put down only $35,000 on that $335,000 house just a year or two ago, and you just got an offer of $370,000! You've just made a profit of $35,000 on your property; you've doubled your invested money in an amazingly short period of time.**)

The problem with leveraging, as with almost everything else in this world, is that it goes both ways: What if the real estate market takes a tumble (as it occasionally does)? A horrific example: In the mid-1980s, a group of magnificent townhouses were built just below Casa Loma, that famous faux castle on a hill just above downtown Toronto. They sold for around $1.2 million each when they were first offered to the eager public. The vast majority of buyers, even if they were well-to-do, must have leveraged their purchases, putting down perhaps $200,000 or $400,000 and borrowing the rest as a mortgage. Fair enough, and in the vast majority of cases, a wise move.

But there was a catastrophic collapse of real estate prices, right across the globe, a few short years later. In the mid-1990s, many of those unsold townhouses went on sale for *less than $400,000 each* — a third of their original price. Can you imagine what it must have been like to be living in one of those highly leveraged townhouses, in, say, the year 2000, *still* owing a million dollars to your bank, while your new neighbour just moved in, having paid $400,000 in cash, and owning his town house entirely? The layout is the same, the view the same, the size of the lot the same . . . but not the price!

Life on the Margin

There's another word for leverage, and it's got a scary history. When one borrows to invest, the term more often used is **margin**. Readers with long memories will recall that in the frantic 1920s, just before the Great Depression, millions of North Americans had been "margining" like crazy. **"Buy me 10,000 shares of Consolidated Unlimited at a buck a share!"** they would scream to their brokers over the phone — and then they'd mail in a cheque for only $1,000, because they were allowed to borrow *up to 90%* of the money needed to purchase those shares.

They were "margining" themselves into bankruptcy, poverty, even despair and suicide. When Consolidated Unlimited dropped to a quarter or a dime, as so many stocks did in the frightening months following the Crash of 1929, the margin was "called." The hapless investors found themselves needing to find $9,000 fast; they usually couldn't, of course, and they were ruined. Having to somehow track down $9,000 to finish paying for 10,000 shares that are now worth a thousand dollars — it's almost a dictionary definition of the phrase "adding insult to injury."

Wall Street may act strange at times, but it ain't *stupid*. Rules were soon passed that set margin limits at 50%. Today, if you want to purchase a thousand shares of promising new Internet stock WebWinner.com at $25 a share, you must put up at least $12,500; you can borrow the other half, no more, on margin from the brokerage. This way, the stock would have to drop by *at least 50%* in price before you would get that dreaded call that led so many people to despair after the great crash of 1929. Of course, if the stock *doubles* in price to $50, congratulations! You have cause to celebrate — you have just made $25,000 (at least on paper) for something that cost you only $12,500 — plus interest charges for your loan, of course. It happens a lot — but hardly all of the time.

Leveraging Can Work Wonders — *If*

Whether you call it "leveraging" or "using margin," *borrowing to invest, whether to purchase a house or quality stocks or mutual funds, is simply a strategy*. It need not be a highly risky one — if, of course, you know exactly what you are doing and what you can afford, and if what you purchase with the borrowed funds has a very good chance of appreciating in value.

Interest rates are important in the world of leveraging and margin. For instance, if it will cost you 12% a year to borrow money from a bank to buy a stock, then the equity would have to go up quite a bit for the leveraging to make any sense. If the stock goes up only 10% over the year — or, heaven forbid, if it drops in value — then the 12% interest you are paying on that loan-to-invest is money thrown away.

But *if you are leveraging for the long term, for a decent home to live in, or for excellent, trustworthy stocks with superior track records, then it is a strategy that can boost your potential returns by a goodly amount.* And what's more, if you borrow to invest in stocks or mutual funds by using your fully paid-off home as collateral, the interest costs you pay on that leveraging will be tax-deductible. You will essentially be writing off your mortgage payments.

The key, of course, to quote one financial expert, is "to borrow only an amount that you can afford to carry in the long term and where your financial well-being will not be jeopardized if your investments don't work out as planned."

It is essential to keep in mind the downside of this powerful financial tool that can greatly increase your potential returns; it can also greatly increase your potential losses. **Leveraging works to your advantage only when the value of what you invest in with your borrowed funds appreciates.** It is a two-edged sword — don't cut yourself badly and bleed financially to near-death.

Many wise and careful investors bought, using margin, such seemingly superior stocks as Home Depot or Microsoft or Nortel Networks early in 2000, then saw those equities drop 50-80% in value over the following year. Who would have guessed that the market would have punished such magnificent, high-revenue and high-profit companies so harshly?

When you borrow to invest, you've got to be very, very sure of what you are doing. With low interest rates and well-thought-out investments, leveraging could be one of the best ways available to grow a great portfolio and achieve eventual wealth — in the long haul.

The benefits of leveraging can be as great as one can possibly imagine: one can build wealth through using "Other People's Money," or OPM; one can reach their financial goals much faster; and leveraging may also create the possibility of tax deduction for interest costs on that mortgage/loan.

Here is an example of the greatness that can lie in leveraging: Let us make the following assumptions:

1. You have $15,000 available to invest (whether cash, or other investments, such as mutual funds — preferably ETFs!

2. You are able to obtain an average return of 12% a year.

3. You can borrow $30,000 from a bank using their 2:1 loan program (such as TD Bank offers).

So, in merely **six years**, the value of your $15,000 will be worth **$30,000** (as we have seen in the Power of 72), considering that 12% annual **return**. *But since you **borrowed** $30,000 from the bank, you have **actually invested** $45,000. And at the end of those same, half-dozen years, you now have $90,000 in your portfolio!* Pretty good.

How about over **12 years**? The $15,000 alone would now be **up to** $60,000. But thanks to that $30,000 loan you took out, and added **to it, your** $45,000 investment is up to $180,000! **Eighteen years?** $120,000, or **$360,000** — which is better? **Twenty-four years?** You are up to $240,000 **and** $720,000, respectively. And at the end of three decades, at that **same, 12%** annual growth rate, your original $15,000 would be worth $480,000, **which** is pretty impressive. But thanks to the 2:1 "matching loan" from **the bank,** *your original $45,000 investment would make you more than a millionaire:* $1,440,000, to be exact! (I hardly have to remind you that *the interest that you would have to pay on that $30,000 loan is TAX DEDUCTIBLE*, and at 6%, would cost you $150 a month — *more* than covered by the phenomenal power of compound interest over the years! And, naturally, if you **choose to** redeem the investment, that $30,000 loan would have to be repaid.)

There are many other LEVERAGING STRATEGIES, of course; **here is one** more to consider: If you lack any cash, or existing investments, **you can** always try to arrange a "line of credit" at your bank, and invest the **proceeds** in SEGREGATED FUNDS, and/or ETFs. As I showed in **Step 3, above, the** performance of quality Index Funds from many countries have averaged *far more* than the 12% I suggested that you could earn with your $15,000 **invest-** ment matched by a $30,000 loan from a bank. Welcome to the **world of** millionaires.

Money Solutions Leveraging Highlights
  • **Leveraging to invest, like all borrowing, has its risks, so the**
  money had better be invested well.

• Leveraging to invest need not be dangerous or excessively risky.
• Never forget that leveraging our home to invest is tax-deductible, allowing you to write off your mortgage costs.
• Never leverage more than you can safely cover, should your investments take an unexpected turn for the worse.

STEP 7

UNDERSTAND THE POWER OF SYSTEMATIC WITHDRAWAL PLANS (SWP) AND LET THEM WORK FOR YOU

Here, I would like to suggest three letters which could make your life a lot easier: **S, W and P.** They stand for SYSTEMATIC WITHDRAWAL PLANS, and they are probably the least used, yet the most advantageous ways — in tax terms — to cash in one's investments, which you finally wish to do so. When you see how well they work, you may find it hard to believe that they are not as common as cell phones or computers. An SWP is usually defined as "regular payments of income," often monthly, to supplement the needs of an investor. But, oh, they are so much more!

I shared considerable research in **Step 3** of this book, pointing out the folly of Timing the Market; of investing in stocks and mutual funds that trade actively, which triggers huge tax burdens (as well as towering management fees). There is a vicious, negative impact on the growth of your investments when they get caught in an invest/sell/pay taxes/sell/pay taxes cycle. Strategies such as those will guarantee only one thing: that you will fail to preserve your money, much less make any.

The Advantages of an SWP

The **advantages** of an SWP can be huge, since it is such a wise alternative to the kind of invest/sell cycle I just noted. It simply involves *withdrawing specific amounts of money from your pool of investments on a regular basis, while the majority remains in your portfolio, always growing, always increasing.* Nearly every mutual fund company or bank will be happy to set up a SWP for you, and you will quickly discover that it is a quiet, but powerful, strategy that can accomplish many things:

- You will always be minimizing the amount of taxes that you must pay on your gains, because a goodly part of your withdrawal is your principal, which is, of course, tax-free.
- You will avoid the destructive, unworkable absurdity of "timing the market" — forever trying to figure out when it's best to jump in or leap out. *Regular (i.e., "systematic") withdrawals will give you the same benefits as dollar-cost averaging.*
- Your investments will continue to grow! Here is a good example of just how wise SWPs can be for you, and for everyone:
- You make a $100,000 initial investment at the beginning of a year.
- You make a $12,000 annual withdrawal at the end of the year.
- You reinvest all of the dividends.
- Now, watch this return, based on the U.S. Stock Total Return Index for the 20 years ending in June of 2000 (which had a 17.3% annual compound rate; see my notes again on ETFs and investing in the world's Stock Market Indices, above!)

	SYSTEMATIC WITHDRAWAL PLAN	
END OF YEAR	ANNUAL WITHDRAWAL	BALANCE LEFT
1	$12,000	$105,300
2	$12,000	$111,517
3	$12,000	$118,809
4	$12,000	$127,363
5	$12,000	$137,397
6	$12,000	$149,167
7	$12,000	$162,973
8	$12,000	$179,167
9	$12,000	$198,163
10	$12,000	$220,445
11	$12,000	$246,583
12	$12,000	$277,241
13	$12,000	$313,204
14	$12,000	$355,388
15	$12,000	$404,870
16	$12,000	$462,913
17	$12,000	$530,997
18	$12,000	$610,860
19	$12,000	$704,539
20	$12,000	$814,424

The total you have withdrawn over two decades? **$240,000.** Add that, if you will, to the amount you STILL HAVE LEFT in your account? *Over one million dollars.*

Naturally, the above table is a simplification, merely to illustrate the great power and genius behind the Systematic Withdrawal Plan. For instance, although the average compound rate of return was over 17% in the U.S. stock index between 1980 and 2000, there *were* years when it was *better* than 17%, and years when it was "worse." But compared to a GIC, a Canada Savings Bond, or most other "traditional" forms of savings, *what a difference!*

The point, I trust, is clear: one can rejoice in the "magic" of Compound Growth, and, through wise investing and intelligent tax planning — of which swps are a key part — you will definitely be able to enjoy the fruits of your labour — and your children, and their children, will be able to pluck fruit from the same tree, in the years to come. Systematic Withdrawal Plans could well be three of the sweetest, most joyous initials you will come across in your financial life.

Money Solutions swps Highlights
• Systematic Withdrawal Plans are a tax-efficient way to take out regular payments of income from your investments.
• They help you to avoid the dangerous and even disastrous action of Timing the Market, since swps help you to achieve the same benefit as Dollar-Cost Averaging.
• swps are a key part of intelligent tax planning, which can supplement your income in a welcome fashion.

SOME FINAL THOUGHTS

I have just written an entire book dedicated to helping you gain proper **knowledge** — not just random, often incorrect **information** — on the world of financial planning. We've looked at key terms, and at **7 Steps** which I truly believe will help you to RETIRE EARLY AND WEALTHY.

One of the joys of life is "synchronicity." And what could be more in "synch" with my advice shared in this book, than the fact that, *the very day I finished writing these words*, in late February, 2006, *The Globe and Mail* had a entire section dedicated to investing. (*"Report on Alternative Investing"* the 10-pager was called, although I would hardly agree that the following suggestion is "alternative"!)

I found it telling that this story, written by Keith Damsell, was called *"Darlings of the TSX,"* and had the sub-heading *"Three fresh options for investors are the fastest growing business of the Toronto exchange."* One of these "options," not surprisingly, was EXCHANGE TRADED FUNDS. It saddened me to read again what I already knew: that *"the Toronto-Dominion Bank exited the ETF business last year."* (I guess it just didn't make them enough money from selling them; but what about their clients **making more money** and **spending less** on MERs to achieve *their* financial goals?) That left Barclays Global Investors Canada Ltd. the only provider of this extraordinary, yet simple, investing tool. (It is the indirect subsidiary of Barclays PLC, a gigantic company based in the U.K., which markets 17 "iUnit funds" that mirror the performance of a vast range of indexes and asset classes, many of which I listed above, in **Step 3: Learn to invest safely and profitably.**

I here quote from the closing few paragraphs of this fine piece of journalism:

> *Demand is intense. Assets under management top $12-billion, up from about $2-billion in 2002. Costs are low, meaning a greater return for the investor. For example, the annual management expense ratio of the $8.3-billion iUnits S&P/TSX 60 Index Fund is 0.17 per cent of a client's assets under management. In contrast, annual fees for Canadian equity funds range from about 1.5 per cent to as high as 2.9 per cent. ETFs*

are passively managed; returns rise and fall with index per-
formance. Critics contend that a good active manager can
boost returns in a weak market while ETF *investors will be*
stuck with depressed returns. But research indicates that pas-
sive management trumps active management regardless of
market conditions, said Geri James, head of product develop-
ment at Barclays Canada. "On the active side, the fees are the
drag," Ms. James said. "Pretty much in every market most
managers underperform the index after fees."

Oh, yes, indeed. When I read articles such as the one quoted above, I think back on how I have spent nearly half of my life — a quarter-century, in fact — in the Financial Services Industry, as a financial advisor, a student, an educator, an author. I built one of Canada's largest and most successful financial planning organizations. As well, I created one of this country's most successful mutual fund companies.

Over those years, I made many of the financial advisors who worked for my firm, and many hundreds of their clients, into millionaires and multi-millionaires. None of the things that I am listing here are part of any attempt to blow my own horn; I'm merely suggesting that I feel I am highly qualified to share many hard-earned insights with my fellow Canadians.

The only constant in life is change. And what better example of "smart change" is my waking up to — and helping my readers to wake up to — Exchange Traded Funds (ETFs), which were simply not available a dozen years ago. It saddens me, and even angers me, that most financial advisors are simply not up-to-date on ETFs, or on many of the other things I have recommended in the preceding pages. But if we are ever to recognize change, and put it into action, then we must gain new knowledge.

Knowledge is, of course, the key to success in anything, from putting together furniture to learning to program your VCR or cell phone — to investing wisely and well. Yet so many financial planners lack that vital knowledge which they must share with the public, and which our fellow citizens are longing for. I've noted earlier in this text, but it is worth repeating, with some sorrow: *financial organizations usually care far more about maximizing their profit than doing what is right or best for their clients.*

The year 2005 is a good example of what I am talking about: most Canadians who had any money in savings accounts in our Big Five banks, received ZERO interest — while the stock market soared. In other words, bank stocks shot up in value, making billions in profits, while the public got nothing from this. A foreign-based financial institution like ING is now paying 3½% on their savings accounts, while the Big Five of Canada are paying less than 2%! It's simply not fair.

If you are counting on yourself to RETIRE EARLY AND WEALTHY, you must do research, of the kind that I've been offering throughout this book. Yet so much quality research is merely an arm's length away, since Best Mortgage Rates and Highest Interest Rates are listed in most Canadian newspapers — whether you find them in neighbourhood variety stores, or even on the internet (the latter, very often free).

I believe that this book can change your life — financially, and forever. I believe that the tools you need, and the knowledge you need, are in your hands at this very moment. I like to say that *"the best way to predict my future is to create it."* Well, you can do the same, so start now. The earlier you do this, the sooner you can (as I chose to call this book) RETIRE EARLY AND WEALTHY.

Good luck.

David Singh
Toronto
Spring 2006